A 2024 Starting-Point Guide

Lille, France

Including the Nord-Pas-de-Calais Area

Barry Sanders – writing as:

B G Preston

ISBN: 9798874197957

2nd Edition – Updated April 2024

Acknowledgements: The author greatly appreciates Sandra Sanders' contributions. She provided substantial editorial assistance throughout the process.

Photography & Maps: Photos and maps in the Starting-Point Guides are a mixture of those taken by the author and external sources including Shutterstock, Adobe Media, Wikimedia, Google Maps and Google Earth. No photograph in this work should be used without checking with the author first.

[1]

---

[1] This symbol, which is used throughout this guide, is the Lille Coat of Arms.

Contents

Start your exploration in Lille's main square, the
Grand Place (Place du Général de Gaulle)

Preface & Some Suggestions

Introduction:

This Starting-Point guide is intended for travelers who wish to really get to know a city and surrounding area and not just make it one quick stop on a tour through France or Europe. Oriented around the concept of using Lille as a basecamp for several days, this handbook provides guidance on sights both in town and some of the nearby towns.

This is a beautiful city to stroll through and explore.
The "Vieille Bourse" (Old Stock Exchange) near the main square
Photo source: Velvet - Wikimedia Commons

Area Covered in this Guide:

The focus or "starting-point" of this guide is the French city of Lille, which is in the northern area of France near the border with Belgium. The area covered in this book is limited to Lille metro area and popular cities such as Dunkirk, and Arras which are easy to reach for a relaxing daytrip.

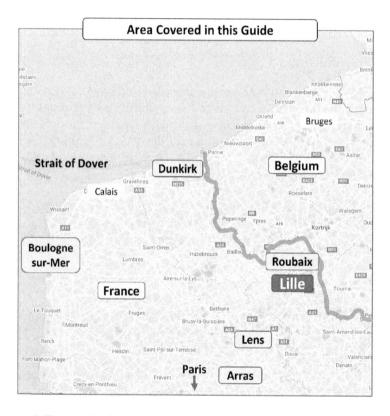

Lille is in the broad area known as Flanders and this section of France is often referred to as French Flanders. The specific name of the French region, of which Lille is the capital, is **Hauts-de-France.** This guide covers some of the highlights of the region and all destinations cited here are easily reached from Lille by train or car in under ninety minutes.

The Ideal Itinerary:

Suggested Duration: If your travel schedule allows **plan on staying 2 to 4 nights in Lille**. This is an area with a wonderful variety of sights outside the town. More than one day is needed to gain even a moderate understanding of what the region has to offer.

A schedule of 3 nights, for example, gives you: (a) an afternoon to explore some of the town on the day you arrive; (b) a full day to explore the sights in Lille; then (c) a day to explore one town such as Dunkirk, plus visit a nearby attraction such as one of the historic battlefields; and finally (d) a departure day to have a relaxing breakfast then head on to your next stop.

Consider a Lille City Pass:

Most cities have discount cards for visitors which can be valuable and reduce hassle if you plan on visiting several attractions. Lille is no exception. The city offers an attractive pass which includes museums and other attractions throughout the area and is not limited to the city of Lille.

In Lille, the pass is referred to as the "Lille City Pass" or "Hello Lille." It is available in 24-, 48- and 72-hour time frames.

These helpful passes will not only provide savings but give you an opportunity to visit area sites of which you might not have been aware. Details on the Lille City Pass may be found in chapter 5 of this guide.

Visit the Tourist Centre:

Lille Tourist Office Website
www.LilleTourism.com

Lille's main tourist center (the Office de Tourisme de Lille) is conveniently located a block south of the Grand Place (Lille's main square) in Place Rihour. This office is also easily reached by taking the city's underground Metro to the Place Rihour station.

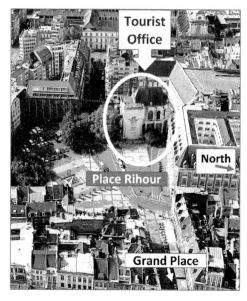

In addition to the office, this agency has a very helpful and complete website. Even if you have done substantial research prior to your trip, it is likely information can be gleaned which had not been previously uncovered.

Also, consider downloading one of the many maps which this office provides as they are quite detailed.

This office will help with:

- Acquiring city passes.
- Booking concerts and shows.
- Obtaining information on local transportation.

4

- Booking tours.
- Providing maps of the town and area.
- Obtaining details on sights to see which meet your preferences.
- Learning about upcoming events.

Obtaining Information on Local Transportation:

Many European cities such as Lille have excellent transportation systems. In the case of Lille and the neighboring communities, there is a good mix of Light Rail (trams), subways, buses, and local trains to take visitors throughout the city and much of the local area.

If you purchase a Lille City Pass, you may ride the local transportation for free.

A Lille "VAL" Metro
Photo source: Jeremy Gunther Heinz - Wikimedia Commons

Understanding this system can be daunting at first. The staff at the tourist office will be able to provide help and transportation maps. See Chapter 6 for guidance on the area's tram and subway system and how to use it. There are also several helpful apps which outline the routes taken, fares, and schedules as shown in the following list.

Download Some Apps:

With the incredible array of apps for Apple and Android devices, almost every detail you will need to have a great trip is available up to and including where to find public toilets. Following are a few recommended by the author.

- **City Pass Lille Métropole**: Lille's City Pass, which includes admission to many museums and other area attractions, has an app to help take full advantage of this pass.

- **Lille Map and Walks:** (Also titled as "GPS My City") Well-rated app with interactive map and details for most area attractions. This firm also provides map-and-walk guides for other cities.

- **Lille Travel Guide:** Another good app which highlights the area attractions along with several interactive guides. An excellent resource for area restaurants and shopping.

- **Lille Metro & Tram Map**: Lille has a comprehensive transportation network. This app goes a long way in helping

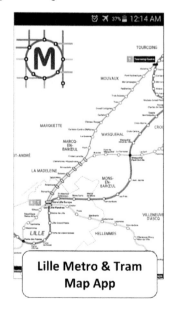

Lille Metro & Tram
Map App

you understand how to use the system and which routes to travel to reach your destinations.

- **Lille Metro Guide and Route Planner**. Like the above Metro and Tram Map app, this provides details on the area's transportation routes.

- **SNCF Trains:** This is the primary train service in France. Use this app to see schedules, routes, and purchase rail tickets for travel into Lille and other cities.

- **Rome2Rio**: An excellent way to research all travel options including rental cars, trains, flying, ferry, and taxi. The app provides the ability to purchase tickets directly online.

- **Trip Advisor**: Probably the best overall app for finding details on most hotels, restaurants, excursions, and attractions.

- **Flush**: A very helpful app which provides guidance on where to find public toilets.

1: Lille Introduction

An Orientation to the City.

Why travel to Lille[2] and the Nord section of France? Simple. With the interesting mix of French, Flemish, and Belgian influences, there is a unique feel to this bustling city. Given the mixture of architecture and cuisine, many people even feel this area should not be part of France at all. At one time, that was the case.

Lille, which is very close to the border with Belgium, has just about everything a traveler could want. There are beautiful and active

The Chamber of Commerce & Belfry towers over central Lille.

---

[2] **Lille Pronunciation:** Stick with the simple <u>"Leel."</u> You may hear some variations on this, but you can't go wrong saying the city name this way. Do <u>not</u> use the typical English pronunciation with a strong "I" – use the "ee" instead of "I"

Lille is not just historic buildings. There are many modern structures in the city center such as the Euralille Towers.
Photo source: Under - Wikimedia Commons

squares, broad avenues, historic buildings, world-class museums, intriguing shopping, and dining spots to sample the area's unique cuisine. In addition to the historical elements of the city, there are many new, strikingly attractive buildings in the modern sectors of town.

Lille was long known as a center of industry and mining. Today, much of that industrial flavor is a thing of the past as the city now focuses on technology, education, and clean industries. Many of the earlier factories, which were notably unattractive, have been torn down and replaced with new centers for business and shopping.

A first-time visitor to Lille would be understandably surprised to find how active and vibrant this city is. For a city with a relatively low profile, it would be easy to mistake it as a more laid-back and smaller city. This is definitely not the case.

9

Lille has numerous broad lanes lined with shops and restaurants such as this one near Place Rihor.
Photo source: Google Maps

For being the fifth largest metro area in France (sixth on some lists), it is not a city which is typically on most visitor's radar from outside of Europe or the region. This can be a good thing as the city is not overrun with tourism and you rarely find large tour groups following flag-toting guides. One big exception to the level of tourism is many individuals come here for short breaks from Paris or England.

When visiting Lille, you will encounter a surprisingly busy city. The level of pedestrian and auto traffic is substantial resulting in a city which provides an active feel. It is not generally a city to come to just to relax and get away from it all.

Lille is on flat land which makes it very easy to explore on foot or bicycle. Most attractions, squares, and historical areas can be reached on foot. When transportation is needed, the area's metro system is superb and easy to navigate.

This is a bicycle-friendly city and bike rental stations may be found throughout Lille and the suburbs.

For war history buffs, Lille makes a good jumping-off point to find museums and battlefields from WWI and some from WWII. Fort Seclin, a WWI fort is on the outskirts of Lille and the coastal areas near Dunkirk and Calais have several notable battlefield monuments.

Some Basic Facts about Lille and it's Region:

- Lille is the capital of France's northern-most region of "Hauts-de-France" which translates to "Heights of France." This is one of the 13 regions of mainland France which were established in 2015 after a consolidation of smaller districts.

- Within the "Hauts-de-France" region, Lille is located in the "Nord Pas de Calais" section which, until 2015, had been a separate region. The differing area names can be confusing at first. For Americans or Canadians, consider the "Hauts-de-France" area to be the rough equivalent of a state within the U.S. or a province within Canada. Then, the smaller "Nord Pas de Calais" area could roughly be thought of as a county.

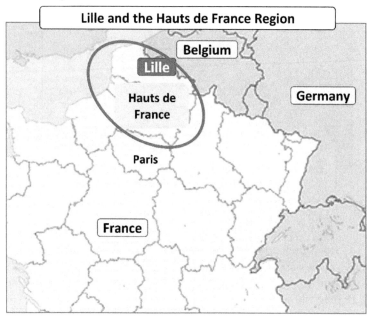

- This region is also called "French Flanders." This is the cultural area which includes the western portions of Belgium. In the 17th century, Flanders was split up with the portion which now contains Lille going to France. Dutch is still spoken by many people in this small area.

- Lille's Population, as of 2019, is 235,000 which makes it the 10th largest city in France. When looking at the metro area, Lille is quite large and spread out. There is a population of almost one and a quarter million people across the metro area, and it is the 5th largest metropolitan area in France.

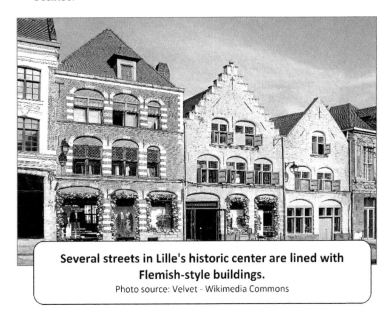

Several streets in Lille's historic center are lined with Flemish-style buildings.
Photo source: Velvet - Wikimedia Commons

- **This is a large college town.** There are over 110,000 full-time students in the metro's universities. Only Paris and Lyon have a greater student population. One aspect of having such a large student population is there is a noticeably young culture with many night spots. The largest university is the University of Lille with roughly 70,000 students.

- **Languages used.** French is by far the most frequently used language in Lille and the area. Even a majority of individuals in neighboring Belgium speak French.

CAUTION
Some older sections of town have cobblestones which can be probablematlc for individuals who are mobility impaired.

Many signs are bilingual in French and Flemish/Dutch. English is spoken by some, especially in the central part of the city. Still, having a few French phrases handy can be helpful.

The General Layout of Central Lille:

Lille is flat with a maze of streets ranging from narrow pedestrian shopping areas to busy boulevards. While the total area of the city is large, most hotels and attractions first-time visitors will go to are in close proximity to the city center. Getting your

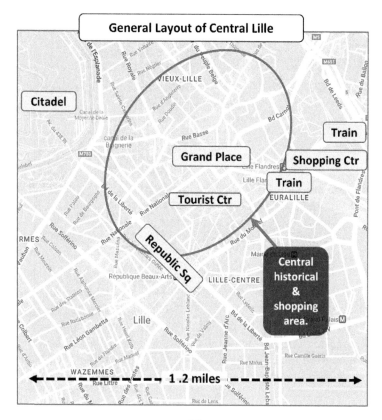

bearings can be a challenge though as streets seem to wander off in random directions without any apparent pattern.

The city's main square, Grand Place or Place du Général de Gaulle, is roughly in the center of the city, and it makes a great starting point for explorations. Some top attractions such as the La Vieille Bourse (Old Stock Exchange) are here. (See chapter 7 for details on this plaza and other attractions in Lille). You will rarely have to walk further than a half-mile (about 1 km) from this plaza to reach a destination.

The older section of town (near the Grand Place) is formally known as "Le Vieux Lille." This is a quaint area of Flemish buildings and numerous shopping lanes.

Much of your explorations of central Lille will be along tree-lined, pedestrian-friendly lanes.
Photo source: Google Maps

A few blocks to the east from the Grand Place is the bustling and modern area of Euralille. This sector of town contains the impressive Westfield Euralille shopping center and both train stations (see chapter 2 for details on the area's train stations).

If you head south from the Grand Place for a 10-minute walk, there is an area defined by a large plaza, the Place de la République, which includes the large Beaux Arts museum (Art Museum).

The last direction to explore out from the Grand Place is west for about a quarter mile (less than a ten-minute walk) is the expansive Citadelle de Lille. This is an historic fortress and park surrounded by canals.

In all cases, the city's excellent network of subways, light rail, and buses will take you close to major sights. This is another great reason to acquire a city pass as it includes transportation. (See chapter 6 for details on this system.)

Some History:

Lille's history, and the history of much of the Nord or Flemish areas of France, dates as far back as 2,000 BC. The area was first inhabited by the Gauls and, over the centuries, other groups such as the Saxons and even the Spanish have played a role in the area's history and development.

Some turning points in the area's history include:

- The Vikings invaded the area in the 9th century and ruled the area for nearly a century.

- Starting in the 11th century the area was formally a part of Flanders. At the time, due in part to mineral wealth, the area was one of the richest in Europe.

- In the 17th century, the area was taken over by the French and Louis the XIV. (Louis the XIV was responsible for building of Versailles).

- Lille's history includes many notable individuals. Charles de Gaulle (for whom the main plaza is named) was born here and Louis Pasteur, noted biologist who created the process of pasteurization, was a professor at the university.

- During the mid-19th century, Lille annexed neighboring towns which are now neighborhoods and suburbs of the city such as the Moulins sector in the southern portion of Lille.

- Lille's modernization really took hold in the last part of the 20th century when a prior industrial area was converted to the Euralille center. This, combined with the high-speed TGV and Eurostar trains put Lille into the position of being a major transportation hub.

Monument to Louis Pasteur in central Lille
Photo source: Wikimedia Commons

- When looking at the impact of major wars on the area, the city was occupied by the Germans in both WWI and WWII. A notable battle took place in the area in WWI with many Canadians and Australians losing their lives.

2: Traveling to Lille

Getting to Lille is not difficult, especially if you are traveling by train. If you are flying, there are a moderate number of flights into this active city. This is not a top tourist destination but is still very easy to reach.

When booking travel to and from here on your own, use trains if possible. The scenery along the way is enjoyable (unless you are crossing under the channel from England and, well, scenery is necessarily limited) and you can travel in a relaxed mode. Curiously, taking the train can often be faster than flying even though the actual transportation time can be longer.

If you choose to fly, the Lille airport is convenient and serviced by a frequent shuttle bus.[3]

Arriving by Train:

Trains are the best way to travel to Lille and many other cities and towns in the region. The stations are near the city center and are often within walking distance of major hotels. Lille has two active train stations (Gares) which are close to each other. Having more than one major station is not the norm for a city of this

---

[3] Flight reductions in France: In an ecological move, France is in the process of reducing flights for routes which are serviced by the high-speed TGV train line. The route from Paris to Lille is among those which are experiencing reduced number of flights.

size. There is, by the way, a very large shopping center between the two train stations which can be handy.

TAKE CARE when planning your travel, especially when departing from Lille. You cannot simply head off to the "main train station" as there are two of them.

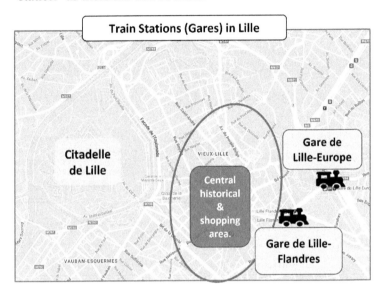

The two primary Train Stations in Lille are:

- Lille Flandres:[4] This station services both local (SNCF) trains and the high-speed trains (TGV). Most local train trips will be from this station, along with some major TGV routes such as central Paris.

---

[4] Flandres: This spelling is easily confused with "Flanders," the name of the region. Flandres is the formal name and spelling for this station.

- **Lille Europe**: This is the first major stop for trains coming in via the "Chunnel" from England on the Eurostar. This station also services the high-speed TGV trains.

Example Train Travel Times to/from Lille		
From	**Avg Travel Time**	**Lille Train Station Used**
Antwerp, Belgium	1 hr 30 min	Lille Europe
Brussels, Belgium	35 min	Lille Europe
Ghent, Belgium	1 hr 15 min	Lille Flandres
London, England	1 hr 25 min	Lille Europe
Paris (City)	1 hr	Lille Flandres
Paris (Airport-CDG)	45 min	Lille Europe
A great travel site to consider: *Rome2rio*	When making your travel plans for travel by train, check out Rome2rio.com. This site provides and compares travel time and costs for: train, driving, and flying.	

Lille's Two Train Stations/Gares
Photo source: Google Earth

Gare Lille Flandres

Euralille Shopping Ctr

Gare Lille Europe

Both of Lille's stations are large and active and very close to the heart of town. Each station is serviced by the area's subway (Metro) and bus systems and access to the stations is clearly marked. Chapter 6 provides further information on this transportation network.

Arriving by Train from Paris:

- Arriving from Paris Airport: A common route for travelers coming from North America is to fly into Paris's Charles de Gaulle airport and then transfer onto a train to Lille.

  It is an easy and enjoyable train ride into the Lille Europe station directly from the Paris airport. There is a sizeable train station directly in the center and lower level of the Charles de Gaulle airport.

  When making flight-to-train connections in CDG (Charles de Gaulle airport), there should be a minimum of sixty minutes (90 is safer) between connections. Most of this time will be needed to get you through airport customs and baggage collection. The time needed to check into your train is minimal. The airport's train station does have a moderate level of security to pass through, although it is generally a quick and non-intrusive process.

  Do not attempt to have bags checked through from your flight to the train. Do plan on gathering your bags at the conclusion of your flight and taking them yourself to the nearby train station.

- If you are traveling to Lille from central Paris, there are high speed TGV trains which take you between the two cities non-stop. You will arrive in the Lille Flandres station. Paris has many train stations, and most trains to Lille depart out of the Gare Nord station which is in the northern section of the city.

  Pay attention to which station from which you will depart Paris. You cannot simply ask a Paris taxi driver to "take me to the train station."

<u>Do not attempt to fly to Lille from Paris</u>. Flights are few and the time involved can be much greater than taking the train.

Arriving by Air:

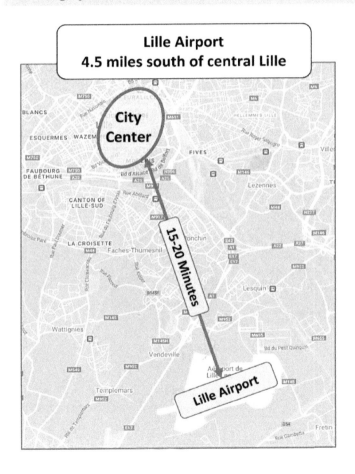

The Lille airport, Aéroport de Lille-Lesquin, is located south of town. It is a 15-to-20-minute drive (much of it along a busy highway) into the heart of Lille. For a regional airport, there is a fair amount of traffic into and out of here with direct flights to not only cities in France, but also to such locations as the Canary Islands, Krakow, Poland, and North Africa.

This is a small and easy airport to navigate so finding your way from the air gate to ground transportation is normally a simple process.

For ground transportation, in addition to taxis and local buses, there is also an airport shuttle which is nonstop from the airport to the two train stations in central Lille. From there, connections to local subways and light rail may be made to finish your journey. Reservations are not needed, and tickets should be purchased directly from the shuttle driver. The cost is 8 Euro each way and the ride takes 20 minutes. They depart once per hour so if you have just missed one, there can be a lengthy wait for the next one. These shuttles will accommodate individuals with limited mobility.

If your hotel is not next to one of the train stations, consider catching a taxi as there is the noteworthy advantage of being taken directly to your lodging and not having to wait for a bus. Cost for a taxi will generally be between 25€ to 40€ plus tip, but this covers everyone who is along for the ride.

3: When to Visit

The climate and moderate tourism in Lille provide a fairly broad time frame for when you can expect to have a pleasant visit. In general, anytime between mid-May to mid-October will provide visitors with acceptable weather (although often wet), popular attractions, and area tours will be open.

Another time to visit Lille is in late April. This is a "shoulder season" with a good blend of moderate tourism, fair weather, and most attractions will be open.

Often a specific event will bring in large crowds. While Lille does have several notable events, the annual Christmas Market is popular and brings in many visitors from the U.K. Lille and the area are likely to be very cold during this time, but the large open market and many decorations make the city a fun place to visit.

Some Seasonal Considerations

Winter: This area can be very cold, wet, and windy so tourism is at a minimum. On the positive side, hotel rates are low so, if your goal is to browse the city's excellent museums or go shopping, then this is a good time to come. Very few tours are operating in the winter. The biggest exception to crowds is the Christmas market, although not a large market as European

Christmas markets go, it is still popular with nearly a million visitors and worth making the trip.

The Lille Christmas Market brings in nearly one million visitors.

Spring: The northern area of France tends to be cool and wet in March and much of April so bring a raincoat. By mid-April, weather will improve although it is frequently rainy. This is another slow period for tourism with not much going on so, as with much of the winter, hotel rates tend to be low. The following table depicts average temperatures and rainfall for each month.

Summer: This is the best time to visit the area. It can be humid and warm but not overly so. The warm weather makes for enjoyable visits to the city parks, outdoor dining, and great adventures to the coast (See chapter 11 for guidance on visiting Dunkirk and the Opal Coast). The downsides to visiting in the summer is an increase in tourism and hotel rates.

Fall: Weather is generally pleasant with cool temperatures. Smaller crowds in October and especially in November. Most tourist-oriented shops and tours will be open through October. Most area tours and attractions will be open into late September or early October and this can be a great time to go to the coast as it will be much less crowded.

Typical Climate by Month:

Average Lille Climate by Month [5]				
Month		Avg High	Avg Low	Avg Rain
Jan	☹	43 F / 6 C	34 F /1 C	2.4 inches
Feb	☹	44 F / 7 C	34 F /1 C	1.9 inches
Mar	😐	51 F /11 C	39 F /4 C	2.3 inches
Apr	😐	57 F /14 C	42 F /5 C	2 inches
May	☺	68 F /20 C	50 F /10 C	2.5 inches
Jun	☺	69 F /21 C	53 F /12 C	2.5 inches
Jul	☺	74 F /23 C	57 F /14 C	2.7 inches

[5] Climate Data Source: Wikipedia.com

Average Lille Climate by Month [5]				
Month		**Avg High**	**Avg Low**	**Avg Rain**
Aug	☺	74 F /23 C	57 F /14 C	2.5 inches
Sep	☺	68 F / 20 C	52 F /11 C	2.4 inches
Oct	☺	59 F /15 C	47 F /8 C	2.6 inches
Nov	😐	50 F /10 C	40 F / 4 C	2.8 inches
Dec	☹	44 F / 6 C	35 F / 2 C	2.7 inches

Major Festivals & Events in Lille & Northern France:

There are several popular events in and near Lille each year. Visiting one of these can be a great addition to a tour of the area especially as many of the events put the area's culture and cuisine on display. The only moderate downsides are the added crowds and increased lodging rates for major events. Information on some of the leading events follow. The website www.LilleTourism.com has comprehensive lists of events, concerts, and festivals around the city and area.

This is not a complete list of all events in and near Lille. The events listed here are some of the more popular ones which have broad appeal.

Winter:

- **Lille Christmas Market:** Nearly one hundred decorated "chalets" showcasing local crafts and cuisine may be found in the city center, primarily around the Grand Place and Place Rihour (the two plazas are close to each other). Lille's shops, main plazas, and streets are brightly lit with Christmas decorations. In addition, there are several concerts, workshops for children, and food tasting events.

  This popular Christmas market begins at the end of November and runs until late December. For specific dates applying to the year you are visiting, check out www.LilleTourism.com then go to the events section. This market runs seven days a week from 11am until 8 or 9pm, depending on the day.

The Dunkirk Carnival is a very lively set of events each winter.
Photo source: Pichasso-Wikimedia Commons

- **Dunkirk Carnival:** The coastal town of Dunkirk holds a large carnival each winter. The exact dates vary but it typically is held over several weekends between mid-January to late February or early March. The carnival has been held for hundreds of years as a tribute to local fisherman. It is purposefully a raucous and lively event with a carnival atmosphere. Join in the fun by dressing in costume and perhaps even participate in one of the many parades.

Dunkirk is easily reached from Lille by train. It is a one-hour train ride. Events are held primarily on the weekends. Details for upcoming carnivals may be found on Dunkirk's tourism site at: www.Dunkirk-Tourism.com.

Spring/Summer:

- **Les Paradis Artificiels:** A popular music festival focusing on current hits and groups. Several performers are brought in each year for the event. Advance ticket purchase is highly required. Held early June at the "Ski Hall," an indoor sports park in the southern section of town. Details on this event may be found at: www.LesParadisArtificiels.fr.

- **Wazemees l'Accordeon:** For something a bit different, consider listening to some of the performances during Lille's annual accordion festival. Despite the name, it is not just about accordion music as a broad range of performers appear. A fun and diverse music festival held in late May to early June. Check out their Facebook page for details.

Fall:

- **Braderie de Lille / Lille Flea Market:** A surprise to many is to learn that Lille's most popular event is a large flea market. By many accounts, it is the largest flea market in Europe. Nearly 2 million people visit this two-day event which is held over one weekend in September each year, typically near the end of the month.

The annual "Braderie de Lille" is Europe's largest flea market.
Photo source: Wikimedia Commons

With a history dating back to the 12th century, this event has really caught on and the streets of Lille are crowded. In addition to the thousands of vendors from across Europe, you will find many enjoyable food stalls promoting local cuisine and numerous musical groups. Details on the event may be found at www.Lille.fr/Braderie-de-Lille.

4: Where to Stay in Lille

Where you choose to stay when visiting a new city is essentially a personal choice. You may prefer hotels or rental apartments, or picking a place guided by your budget may be critical to you.

Regardless of the motives which drive your selection or the type of accommodation you prefer, the "Where in town should I stay?" question is critical to helping you have an enjoyable visit.

Budget and accommodation-type issues aside, the following criteria may be of importance to you:

- Convenience to historical sites, restaurants, shopping.
- Convenience to transportation.
- Noise levels around where you will stay.

> **Author's Recommendation:**
>
> Stay in the area roughly outlined by the Grand Place and Gare Flandres.

This guide does not provide details on all of Lille's hotels. There are many fine and dynamic online sources such as Trip Advisor, Booking.com, and others which provide far more detail than can be provided here. These sites will provide answers to every question you may have about a property and allow you to make reservations once you have made your selection.

Outlined here are two sections of town to consider for accommodations when planning your trip. This is far from a

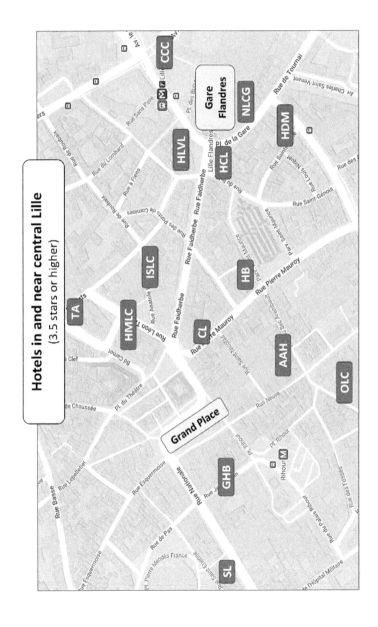

Hotels in and near central Lille
(3.5 stars or higher)

complete list, but for a first-time visit, staying in one of these areas is suggested. [6]

There are several areas and hotels outside of these suggested locations, but they often do not provide the easy access to local attractions and transportation.

Hôtel Mercure Lille Centre Grand Place
One of several well-rated hotels closee to the Grand Place
Photo source: AllAccor.com

---

[6] Hotel Ratings & Rates: All hotel ratings cited in this chapter are a blend of several sources such as: author experience, Booking.com, Trip Advisor, and others as of mid-2024. Fares (cost per night) are not indicated in this guide as they can vary dramatically by the time of year and type of room selected. Check your preferred booking site such as the hotel's website, Trip Advisor, Booking.com, and others for rates at the time you will be staying in Lille.

Area Near Gare Flandres & Grand Place:

There are some positives to staying in this area of town including easy access to transportation, proximity to many of the city's leading attractions, and a wide array of restaurants and shops.

Hotels to Consider in Central Lille			
Note: there are many hotels and inns in this section of town. The following list is a representative sample only. Map Codes cited are from the map near the start of this chapter.			
Map Code	Hotel Name	Rating	Website
AAH	Arembault Appart Hôtel	3.5	Arembault-Appart-Hotel.fr
CCC	Citadines City Centre	3.5	DiscoverASR.com
CL	Hôtel Carlton Lille	4.5	CarltonLille.com
GHB	Grand Hôtel Bellevue	4	GrandHotelBellevue.com
HB	Hôtel Brueghel	3.5	Hotel-Brueghel.com
HCL	Hôtel Chagnot Lille	3.5	Hotel-Chagnot-Lille.com
HDM	Hôtel du Moulin d'Or Lille	3.5	HotelMoulin-dor.com
HLVL	Hôtel La Valiz Lille	3.5	HotelLaValiz.com
ISLC	Ibis Styles Lille Centre Grand-Place	4	All.Accor.com (Then search for Lille)

Hotels to Consider in Central Lille			
Note: there are many hotels and inns in this section of town. The following list is a representative sample only. Map Codes cited are from the map near the start of this chapter.			
Map Code	**Hotel Name**	**Rating**	**Website**
HMLC	Hôtel Mercure Lille Centre Grand-Place	4.5	
NLCG	Novatel Lille Centre Gares	4	
OLC	Okko Hotels Lille Centre	4.5	OkkoHotels.com
SL	Sparadise Lille	4	SparadiseLille.com
TA	The Appart	3.5	TheAppart.fr

Adjacent to Euralille and Gare Lille Europe:

Next to, and somewhat overlapping, the previously de-scribed area is a collection of some of the largest and highest-rated hotels in the city. The Euralille area of town contains the busy "Gare Lille Europe" train station and the very large West-field shopping center.

Although this area has a greater walk into the heart of town than the sector between Gare Flandres and the Grand Plaza, it is easy to catch the subway (Metro) from here into town or stroll the large mall. If you are taking an early train, staying in one of these properties can be ideal as the stations are in the immediate vicinity.

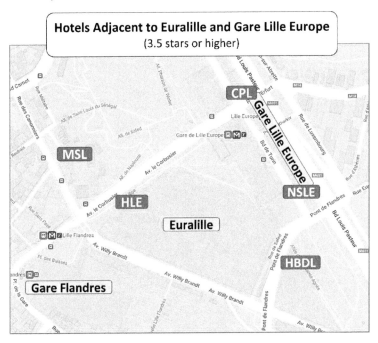

Hotels Adjacent to Euralille and Gare Lille Europe
(3.5 stars or higher)

Hotels near Euralille and Gare Lille Europe			
Map Codes cites are from the map preceding this table.			
Map Code	Hotel Name	Rating	Website
CPL	Crowne Plaza Lille-Euralille	4	IHG.com (Then search for Lille)
HBDL	Hôtel Barrière	4.5	HotelBarriere.com
HLE	Hôtel Lille Europe-Euralille	3.5	Hotel-Lille-Europe.com

Hotels near Euralille and Gare Lille Europe

Map Codes cites are from the map preceding this table.

Map Code	Hotel Name	Rating	Website
MSL	Mama Shelter Lille	3.5	Fr.MamaShelter.com
NSLE	Novatel Suites Gare Lille Europe	4	AccorHotels.com (Then search for Lille)

The large Crowne Plaza Hotel is next to the Gare Lille Europe train station.
Photo source: IHG.com

5: Lille City Pass

Like most cities in Europe, Lille offers a pass which provides easy access to local attractions such as area museums. This pass also includes transportation on the city and area's transportation network.

The official name of this offering is the "City Pass Métropole Européenne de Lille." If you will be staying in Lille or the area, and devoting multiple days to activities in this city, you should consider purchasing one of the available passes. The primary reason to do so is cost savings. If you only want to visit one or two sights, then purchasing a pass is probably not warranted.

Full details on the city pass may be found on the CityPass.LilleMoetopole.fr website.

This pass is available in printed form and as an app. If you acquire the app from either the Apple or Android store, it has added value of providing an interactive map.

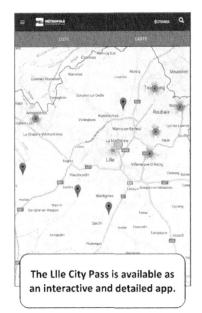

The Llle City Pass is available as an interactive and detailed app.

Pass Options and Fees:

There are three variations of the Lille City Pass based on the amount of time it will be valid. **24-, 48-, and 72-hour passes.** In each case, the time for using a pass starts with its first use – not at the start of a specific day. So, for instance, if you buy a 48-hour pass and you first use it at noon on a Monday, then it is valid until noon on Wednesday.

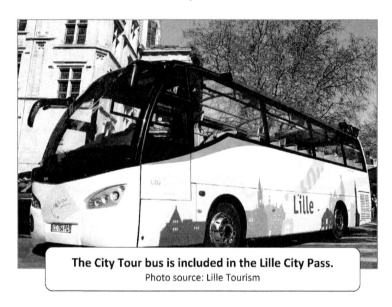

The City Tour bus is included in the Lille City Pass.
Photo source: Lille Tourism

The 24- and 48-hour passes are focused on attractions within Lille and neighboring towns within the area roughly defined as the Lille Metropolis. Details of attractions included follow, but in essence, they cover nearly 30 attractions, plus free local transportation. The passes also include several area discounts for shopping and dining.

The 72-hour pass includes all that is within the 24- or 48-hour passes, but also includes 14 attractions in the Nord-Pas de Calais region. Another advantage is it includes transportation on the local train network (SNCF) in addition to transportation within Lille.

Pass Costs and Where to Purchase: The Lille City Pass may be purchased online, from the tourist office in Lille or from one of several online vendors. If your schedule allows, consider holding off to purchase your passes until you arrive in Lille and can go to the Tourist Office. There are many advantages to do so including the office providing local assistance and local maps.

If you wish to purchase the pass online, the best source is to do so is directly from the LilleTourism.com website. When  this is done there is a 10% reduction in the cost, however this is offset with shipping costs which more than outweigh the discount provided. The passes may also be purchased online from providers such as Viator.com or GetYourGuide.com.

Pass Pricing:[7]

- 24-hour: 25€
- 48-hour 35€ -avg of 17,50€ per day.
- 72-hour 45€-avg of 15€ per day

---

[7] **Pass Price Note:** These are the full rates without any online discount as of April 2024. Prices are subject to change.

What the Passes Cover:

Passes provide much more than free entrance to museums and other noted attractions. One of the biggest benefits is free use of local transportation. You will also be eligible for several local tours, such as the city tour bus. The following table details many of the items included within these Lille City Passes. The list is subject to change.

One note of caution. Many attractions which are cited as being in the Lille Metropolitan area are not immediately within central Lille. Many of them are in nearby towns/suburbs which can take some travel to reach them. Take note in the following tables of the town where each attraction is located. Using the City Pass app can greatly help in determining where an attraction is located and if you want to make the trek out to it.

> Details on many of the museums and attractions covered in these passes may be found in chapter 5 of this guide.

Attractions Included in all Lille City Passes.		
(Partial Listing)		
Type Of Attraction	**Attraction**	**Where Located**
Transportation & Tours	Lille buses, Metro, and Light Rail	Lille Metro Area
	City Tour Bus	Central Lille
	Guided Walking Tour of Old Lille	Central Lille
	Belfrey of Hôtel de Ville Tour	Central Lille
Fine Arts	Palais Des Beaux-Arts	Central Lille

Attractions Included in all Lille City Passes. (Partial Listing)		
Type Of Attraction	**Attraction**	**Where Located**
(art icon)	Arts Museum	
	La Piscine Art Museum	Roubaix
	Le Fresnoy Contemporary Art Museum	Tourcoing
Science & Technology (science flask icon)	Musée d'Histoire Naturelle Natural History Museum	Central Lille
	Musée de L'Institut Pasteur Pasteur Institute Museum	Central Lille
	Forum Départmental des Sciences Astronomy & Science Museum	Villeneuve-d'Ascq
	La Manufacture Musée Textiles Manufacturing Museum	Roubaix
History (building icon)	La Condition Publique Textiles & Design	Roubaix
	Maison Natale Charles de Gaulle Birthplace of Charles de Gaulle	Central Lille
	Maison Folie Hospice D'Havre Convent and college	Tourcoing
	Fort de Seclin Fort built during Franco-Prussian War	Seclin
	Les Prés du Hem	Armentières

Attractions Included in all Lille City Passes.		
(Partial Listing)		
Type Of Attraction	Attraction	Where Located
Parks & Gardens 	Large park and recreation area	
	Musée de Plein Air Open air museum & park	Villeneuve d'Ascq
	Mosaïc le Jardin des Cultures The Garden of Cultures	Moquet

The 72-Hour Lille City Pass:

If you will be in Lille for several days and are likely to travel to the coast or other areas in the region, consider acquiring the longer 72-hour pass as it includes an additional 14 attractions plus greater travel benefits.

All of these added attractions are outside of Lille and will require travel by train or car to reach them.

The Louvre Museum has a branch in the town of Lens. This museum is included in the 72-hour Lille City Pass.
Source: Dalbéra-Wikimedia Commons

Additional Items included in the 72-hour Pass		
(Partial Listing)		
Type Of Attraction	Attraction	Where Located
Transportation & Tours	Free use of regional train network. The SNCF trains throughout the Nord-Pas de Calais area.	Area wide.
	Les Bateaux Promenades du Vieux Douai Boat tour along the canals of the town of Douai	Douai
Museums & Memorials	Musée de Louvre Lens Satellite site to the famed Louvre Museum in Paris.	Lens
	Musée Matisse Matise Art and History Museum	Le Cateau-Cambrésis
	Musée Portuaire Dunkerque Harbor & Shipping Museum	Dunkirk
	Mémorial 14-18 Notre-Dame-De-Lorette WWI Museum and Monument	Souchez
	La Carrière Wellington WWI Memorial and Tunnels	Arras
	Musée de Flandre Flanders Art & History Museum	Flanders

Additional Items included in the 72-hour Pass		
(Partial Listing)		
Type Of Attraction	Attraction	Where Located
Other Attractions	Les Boves Underground tour of Arras	Arras
	Le Beffroi de Saint-Eloi Climb to top of the church belfry at the Dunkirk cathedral.	Dunkirk

View of Dunkirk/Dunkerque from bell tower at the Saint-Éloi cathedral is included in the Lille 72-hour pass.

6: Lille's Transportation System

Subways, light rail, buses, and bicycles. Lille has a comprehensive transportation network that includes all of these modes of travel and covers an area expanding well beyond the city center.

The Metro system "Métro de Lille Métropole" operates both above and below ground.

The Metro (subway) portion of Lille's transportation network covers 60 stops over two lines. In total distance, it is the second longest system in France with only Paris being longer. These lines are generally underground in the city center and at or above ground further out.

Having only two Metro/subway routes in the city center makes learning how to navigate the system fairly easy. Still, given that these two lines tend to twist about and cross each other, some confusion can arise. Luckily, clear maps of the system are displayed at every stop and several helpful apps are available.

The system is much more than the two Metro lines, their "VAL" system[8]. There are also numerous bus routes, a light rail system, and even several local and regional train stations which, for newcomers, can be confusing. Again, this is where having an app available can be very helpful.

When traveling in the heart of Lille, most public transport will be done on buses or on the Metro. The light rail system only comes into play when traveling north to the major suburbs such as the attractive towns of Tourcoing or Roubaix. These two towns are part of the expansive Lille metropolitan area and next to the border with Belgium.

Use one of the Lille transportation apps to help navigate the system.

Two maps follow. The first provides an overview of the Metro and light rail system close to central Lille, and the second map provides a birds-eye view of the whole Metro and light rail network. Not shown on these maps are the numerous bus lines and regional rail stations. Most regional rail stations are on the outskirts of town with the notable exception of Gare Flandres which connects travelers to most modes of travel.

---

[8] **VAL System:** This is an acronym for the French-named transportation system of "Véhicule Automatique Léger."

All metro lines and the light rail line trains connect to both Gare Flandres and Gare Lille Europe.

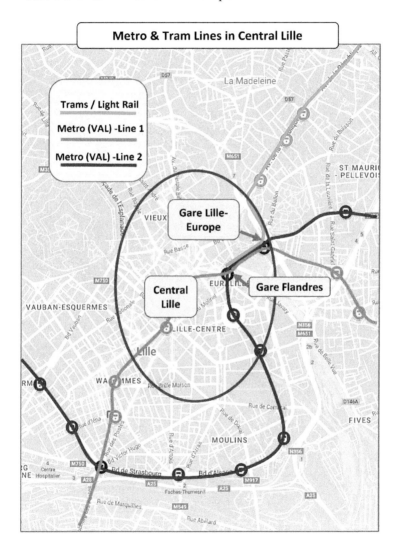

The Metro and light rail network is expansive and takes riders close to the Belgium border.

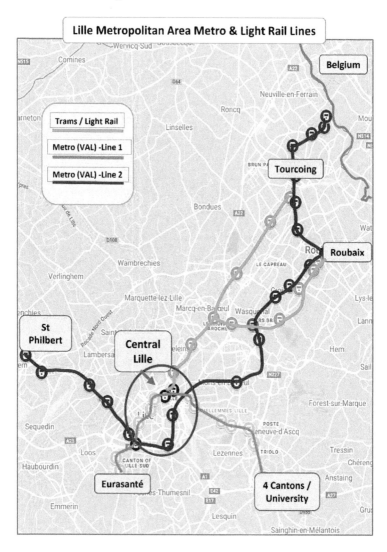

Purchasing Transportation Tickets:

The best way to purchase tickets for any local transportation is from one of the ticket dispensers found at every metro and light rail stop and most bus stops. You may also purchase passes online if you download the Lille Metro app, but this is generally not needed unless you will be in town for an extended period.

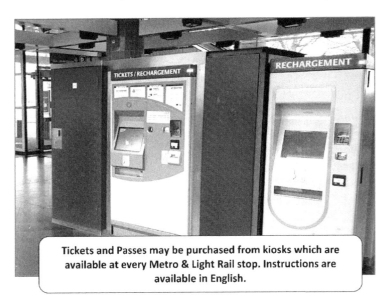

Tickets and Passes may be purchased from kiosks which are available at every Metro & Light Rail stop. Instructions are available in English.

Purchasing tickets is easy and several variations are available. The same tickets are used for buses, subways, and light rail.

- One-way ticket – regardless of distance: 1,80€ [9]
- Packet of 10 one-way tickets – any distance: 15.40€

---

[9] **Ticket Purchase Prices:** All costs cited here are as of mid-2024 and are subject to change.

- Short Ride – limited to distance of 3 stops: 1,15€

- Day Pass – unlimited travel for a 24-hour period: 5,30 €

Once you have purchased a pass, it then needs to be validated at one of the machines which is located at the entrance to every metro or light rail stop.

> Keep in mind that Lille public transportation is free if you have a Lille City Pass.

Bicycle Rental:

Much of Lille can easily be explored on bicycle and, with a large network of bike trails and routes, it is easy to do. Lille's bicycle program is quite large with a network of over 220 self-serve stations and over 1,800 bikes. This program, V'Lille, is operated by the same firm which runs the local transportation network.

> V'Lille -Cycl'lille App
> Download and use the app to locate rental stations and rent bikes. (Caution -French Language only)

The V'Lille program allows you to simply rent a bike from one of the numerous stations and return it at any point in time to any station of your choosing.

Two cautions: (a) the fee is based on the time you keep the bike, so don't plan on retaining a specific bike overnight or for several days as a noteworthy security deposit will be charged, and (b) when returning a bike, there must be an available docking slot. If not, you will need to locate another rental station to return your bike. If you use the app, it will identify which rental locations have available bikes and docking stations to return the bike.

V'Lille stations are frequently next to Metro and light rail stations which adds to the convenience.

V'Lille bicycle rental stations may be found near metro and light rail stops in addition to numerous other locations.
Photo Source: Google Maps

<u>V'Lille Bike Rental Rates:</u> When first looking at the rate structure for the V'Lille bike sharing system in Lille, it can be a bit confusing. There are essentially two parts to this. The first is a "subscription fee" of 1,75€ for a 24-hour period (other time frames are available). This gives you the right to use bikes for up to thirty minutes at no charge as often as you like during this time frame.

On top of the subscription fee is the second part – a usage fee of 1 Euro for every thirty minutes after the free 30-minute period.

At first, when looking at these fees, it is reasonable to ask which is the fee, the 1,75€ for 24-hours or the 1€ fee for 30-minutes. The simple answer is both.

To enable rentals, your first step is to set up the subscription and provide your credit card information. This may be done via the app or any of the kiosks at the rental stations. At this time, you are provided via a text or e-mail (your choice) a code which is good for 24-hours. Use this code when retrieving a bike from one of the hundreds of available rental stands.

A third, refundable fee of 200€ is charged when setting up your account. It will not be charged unless you do not return your bike within 24 hours.

7: Points of Interest in Central Lille

The variety of attractions in and near Lille are quite diverse and spread over a broad area, not just in the city's center. Chapter 8 details several popular attractions just outside of Lille's center. This does not mean that you will need to hop aboard a local metro or bus to the area's major features. Within the historical center or "Centre Ville," there are many attractions of note ranging from impressive museums, historical buildings, and expansive parks. All are within a reasonable walking distance.

A great place to start your explorations is the notable and very photogenic square of "Grand Place" which is more formally referred to as "Place Charles de Gaulle." From here, you can easily travel out to view the city's major attractions. Also, the Tourist Office, "Office de Tourisme de Lille," is just a block south of the Grand Place. This office can book any number of tours for you or simply provide local maps and helpful guidance.

> ### Consider a Walking Tour
> Visit the tourist office to book a local walking tour. Some are free and all will help you understand this historic city.

Information on several of central Lille's most popular destinations follow. This list does not include the more popular shopping and dining venues as they are detailed in a later chapter.

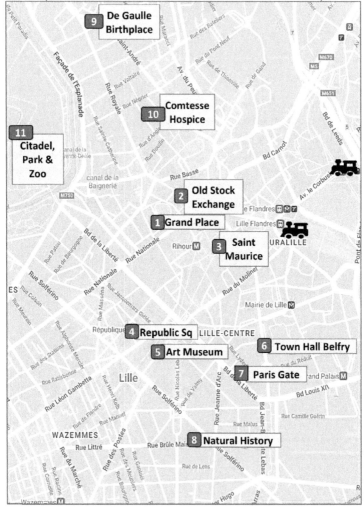

Points of Interest in Central Lille

Map Numbers are used to identify following descriptions.

9 De Gaulle Birthplace

10 Comtesse Hospice

11 Citadel, Park & Zoo

2 Old Stock Exchange

1 Grand Place

3 Saint Maurice

4 Republic Sq

5 Art Museum

6 Town Hall Belfry

7 Paris Gate

8 Natural History

The Grand Place area is home to many historically significant buildings.
Photo source: Google Earth

Théâtre du Nord

Old Stock Exchange

Opéra de Lille

Grand Place

Chamber of Commerce & Belfry

1 - Grand Place / Place du Général-de-Gaulle :

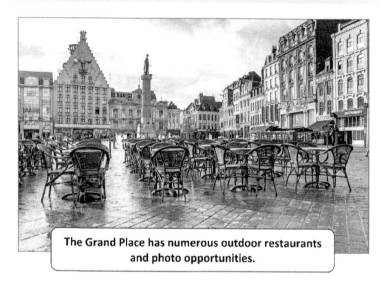

The Grand Place has numerous outdoor restaurants and photo opportunities.

Description: This historic main square of Lille started as a market area in the 14th century. Originally, this square was much larger, but in the 17th century, the old stock exchange (Vielle Bourse) divided it into two sections with the Grand Place being the larger open portion. The other remining open plaza left after the building of the Old Stock Exchange is the Place du Théâtre.

The square is bordered by several historic buildings in addition to the Old Stock Exchange and several are listed as historical monuments such as North Theater. In the center of the square, is a prominent statue, the "Column of the Goddesses." This statue was built in 1845 to honor the

If you can visit only one section of Lille, this square and the adjoining historic buildings should be it.

citizens of Lille who fought in a battle in the late 18th century, the Siege of Lille.

The Grand Place square received the formal name of "Place du Général-de-Gaulle after WWII as an honor bestowed on Charles de Gaulle. Even with this name change, the term "Grand Place" is still commonly used.

Today, this is the center of activity for fairs, the popular "Braderie de Lille" (A huge flea market each September), the winter fair, and many other events. Several shops and restaurants line the plaza making this an easy and enjoyable spot to relax, dine and watch the comings-and-goings.

Getting Here: For as prominent as this plaza is, it is a bit surprising to learn there is no Metro stop here. The closest metro stop is at Place Rihour (the same plaza which houses the tourist office). This is a short 1-block walk.

If you are driving, there is a parking area under the plaza.

2 - Old Stock Exchange / Vielle Bourse de Lille:

Description: One of Lille's most iconic buildings, this large structure lines the Grand Place and is hard to miss. It is an excellent example of Flemish architecture from the 17th century, even though it was built when the area was held by Spain and under Spanish influence.

The ornate structure is actually made up of 24 homes which are located around an open, arched courtyard.

Markets are often held in the building's courtyard with a used book market being one of the more frequent and common. Visitors are limited to viewing the exterior of the building as no tours are provided of the interior.

**Open Courtyard in the Old Stock Exchange /
"Vielle Bourse de Lille"**

Getting Here: This structure is between the two popular squares of Grand Place and the Place du Théâtre. The closest Metro stop is at Place Rihour, just a short walk south or stroll over to Gare Lille Flandres and the metro stop there. The walk to Gare Flandres takes slightly under ten minutes.

3 - Saint Maurice Church / Église Saint-Maurice:

Description: A large Gothic church was constructed starting in the 14th century and finished in the 19th century. Its architecture is in a style unique to the Flanders region called the "Hallekerque" style meaning "Barn Like." It has been named a "Monument Historique."

The church is free to visit. Inside are several historically significant stained-glass windows which were crafted in the late 17th century and early 18th century. The central portion of the chapel contains a long nave with several bays for choir and several small side chapels. All sights open to visitors are on one, easy to explore level.

Exterior of Saint Maruice Catholic Church
Église Saint-Maurice de Lille

Getting Here: The location is a 4-minute walk southeast from the Grand Place and roughly midway between the Grand Place and Gare Lille Flandres. The closest metro stop is at Gare Flandres.

4 - Republic Square / Place de la République:

Description: One of Lille's largest open spaces (larger than Grand Place), it was created on old fortifications in the mid-19th century. This relaxing square is bordered by the impressive "Prefecture of Lille" (an administrative complex) and the large art museum, the "Palais des Beaux Arts."

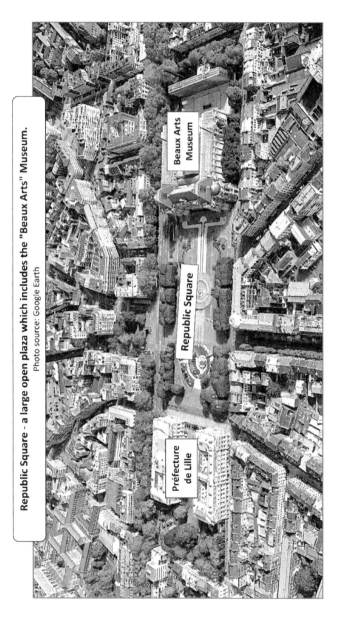

Republic Square - a large open plaza which includes the "Beaux Arts" Museum.

Photo source: Google Earth

Beaux Arts Museum

Republic Square

Préfecture de Lille

In the square, is an open-air amphitheater which is used for numerous small events. There is also an impressive fountain with a large pool and water jets. For initial visitors to Lille, a good reason to come here is to find a relaxing and open place in the center of the city and a great rest stop before (or after) viewing the expansive Beaux Arts museum.

Getting Here: There is a Metro stop under the plaza allowing for easy transit to here. Take the M1 line and get off at République Beaux-Arts stop. If you are driving, there is a parking garage under the plaza.

5 - Art Museum / Palais des Beaux-Arts de Lille:

Description: Most cities in France have a "Beaux Arts" museum (fine arts museum) with impressive collections and Lille is no exception.

One of the largest art museums in France, this expansive facility was built in the 19th century. The current museum (it had previously been located elsewhere) is built in what is called the "Belle-Époque" stye. This is term, which generally relates to the period of the late 19th century, was focused on cultural refinement.

"Birth of Venus"
by Amaury Duval.
One of many treasures in the Lille Beaux Arts Museum.
Source: Wikimedia Commons

Visitors to this beautiful museum will find a comprehensive collection of art and sculpture from the Renaissance, Middle Ages, and earlier. The museum's collection holds over 70,000 pieces.

The "Palais des Beaux-Arts de Lille" on Republic Square

Entry Fees: If you hold a Lille City Pass, there is no fee to enter. Full adult rate is 7€ and child and senior rates are 4€. Extra fees apply for special exhibits and workshops. See chapter 5 for details on the Lille City Pass and the benefits it provides.

Hours: Closed on Tuesdays. Monday has shortened hours of 2pm to 6pm. All other days the museum is open from 10am to 6pm.

Website: **pba.Lille.fr**

Getting Here: Take the metro M1 to the République Beaux-Arts station. Or, if you are driving, there is parking under Republic Square. If you prefer to walk, it is roughly a 10-minute trek from the area of Grand Place.

~ ~ ~ ~ ~ ~

6 - Town Hall Belfry / Beffroi de l'Hôtel de Ville:[10]

A ten-minute walk southeast from the Grand Place is an impressive structure which dominates the city's skyline. The Town Hall Belfry (Beffroi de l'Hôtel de Ville) stands over 340 feet, (104 meters) and is the tallest such belfry in France.

During WWI, the city's existing belfry was destroyed, and this new structure was put in place and opened in 1932. It is now classified as a UNESCO World Heritage Site.

Observation Platform

Lille Town Hall Belfry
Photo Source: Remih-Wikimedia Commons

Visitors may travel up to the observation tower near the top and enjoy great views of the city in all directions. CAUTION, the trip can be arduous and is not geared to individuals with limited mobility. There is an elevator, but it is not always available so plan on the potential of having to hike the 110 steps to the top.

It is best to make reservations in advance, especially in high season, as this tower is one of the area's most visited attractions.

---

[10] Hôtel de Ville: This is not a hotel. The term can be confusing to individuals who have not visited much of France. It is used in cities throughout the country to identify the town hall and not any sort of lodging establishment.

During the tour, there are several historical plaques. Also note that, for security reasons, entrance is restricted, and you must first ring a bell at the entry door and wait to be admitted.

Entry Fees: If you hold a Lille City Pass, there is no fee to enter. Full adult fee is 7,.50€. If you make a reservation online, a discount is provided. Tickets may also be purchased from several online resellers such as Viator.com and GetYourGuide.com. The fee is roughly $11USD per person.

Hours: Closed on Monday and Tuesday. Operating hours are split into two portions: morning from 10am to 1pm and afternoon from 2pm to 5:30pm. Reservations via the LilleTourism.com site are highly recommended. The morning session is generally limited to individuals with advance reservation.

Website: **LilleTourism.com** (Then navigate to the page for this attraction).

Getting Here: Take the metro line M2 to the Lille Grand Palais or the Marie de Lille station then walk 5 minutes to the Hôtel de Ville and the Belfry. While here, consider stopping in to visit the Pasteur Museum[11] and the Natural History Museum. Both are quite close to this metro stop.

7 - Paris Gate / Porte de Paris Monument:

A masterpiece of military architecture, the Porte de Paris is the only remaining city gate in Lille from 17th century fortifications. When the French took back the region from the Spanish Kingdom, a set of fortified walls and gates were built around the city of Lille. Today, this ornate structure is all that remains of the fortifications. It has remained as an historic monument and is

---

[11] Pasteur Museum: The "Musée de L'Institut Pasteur de Lille" is only open for limited hours on the weekends and is a small specialty museum. Further information may be found at **Pasteur-Lille.Fr.**

surrounded by a small set of formal gardens. At the top, are statues of two angels, Mars and Hercules. These two statues represent war and strength.

Paris Gate / Porte de Paris Monument
Town Hall Belfry in the background.

Visitors are not allowed to go up into the structure, but just
viewing it and the gardens is inspiring. Nearby, are the Town
Hall Belfry and the Lille Natural History Museum.

<u>Getting Here:</u> Take the metro line M2 to the Lille Grand Palais
station.

8 - Natural History Museum:

> **Great Destination for Children**
> Many displays and activities are geared to children here.

This is one of the oldest and largest
natural history museums in France. It
started in the early 19th century with a
collection of amateur zoological find-
ings and has greatly expanded since.
Now in its 150th year, the museum has
acquired specimens from every corner

of the globe. There are large collections of amber with trapped insects, skeletons from exotic and ancient species, and much more.

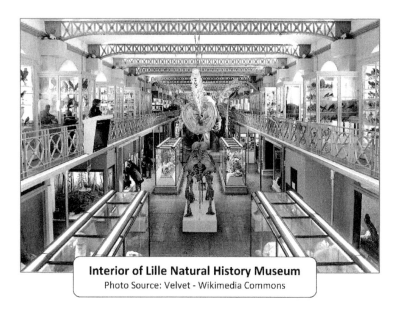

Interior of Lille Natural History Museum
Photo Source: Velvet - Wikimedia Commons

Entry Fees: Included in the Lille City Pass. Without a pass, normal fees are 3,80€ for adult. If there is a major exhibition, the entry fee is 5 Euro. Reservations may be purchased online from the museum's website. This site also provides the ability to book guided tours.

Hours: Closed on Tuesday. Operating hours are 9:30am to 5pm on the weekdays and open 10am to 6pm on weekends.

Website: **MNH.Lille.fr**

Getting Here: Take the metro line to either the Marie de Lille or the République Beaux Arts station. From either of these Metro stops, it is roughly a 10-minute walk.

9 - De Gaulle Museum:

Tucked away on a quiet side street in a residential area is the birthplace of Charles de Gaulle, one of France's most noted 20th century leaders. After a successful military and diplomatic career, he became the President of France in 1959 and held the office for a decade. While he was born in Lille, most of his early years were in Paris where his father worked as a teacher.

Charles de Gaulle Birthplace & Museum
Photo Source: Velvet - Wikimedia Commons

Today, the "Maison Natale" for Charles de Gaulle is set up to give the sense of what the home would have been like when he was born in the late 19th century. There is more here than just his home. Adjacent to the home is the Charles de Gaulle Museum which provides history of the area and historical documents.

When visiting the museum, take note that it is in a residential area and there is little here in the way of services or restaurants.

<u>Entry Fees:</u> Included in the Lille City Pass. Without a pass, normal fees are 6€ for adult. Reservations are recommended during high season, via the website and phone, due to limited capacity.

<u>Hours:</u> Closed on Tuesday. Normal operating hours are 10am to 6pm.

<u>Website:</u> **MaisonDeGaulle.fr**

<u>Getting Here:</u> The address is 9 rue Princesse, 59000 Lille.

There is no metro stop nearby and walking distance to the Grand Place is nearly 20 minutes each way. Should you choose to walk, it is easy to stop in at the Comtesse Hospice Museum as it is mid-way along the route. If you wish to take the bus, the closest stop to De Gaule Museum is served by line 9.

10 - Comtesse Hospice / Musée de l'Hospice Comtesse:

Founded by the Countess Flandres (the same spelling as Gare Flandres) in the 13th century as a hospital, this set of buildings remained as a working hospice until 1939. Crafted in the

Comtesse Hospice Museum
Photo Source: Patrick - Wikimedia Commons

Flemish style, this is an interesting way to experience aspects of Lille's history. The rooms are furnished much as they were in earlier centuries when this was run by Augustine nuns. Numerous paintings, sculptures, and porcelain items from the region are on display. In addition to the old hospital wards, take time to explore the formal gardens and courtyards.

Entry Fees: Included in the Lille City Pass. Normal fees are 3,70€ for adult. (All fees cited in this guide are subject to change.)

Hours: Closed on Tuesday. It is open on Monday in the afternoons from 2pm to 6pm. Wednesday to Saturday, it is open a full day from 10am to 6pm.

Website: **mhc.lille.fr**

Getting Here: The address is 32 rue de la Monnale, 59000, Lille. There are no Metro stops nearby. It is an easy 6-to-8-minute walk from Grand Place. If you wish to take a bus, the nearest stop is at Palais Justice.

11 - The Citadel Park & Zoo / Parc de la Citadelle:

In the northwest section of central Lille, is a large complex with a 17th century fort as its centerpiece. The Lille Citadel (Citadelle de Lille) is surrounded by a 270-acre (110 hectare) park, the Parc de la Citadelle.

There is something here for everyone and it is easy to spend a full day exploring and relaxing.

Lille Citadel / Citadelle de Lille: Constructed in the shape of a pentagon in 1670, this bastion was built under the orders of Louis XIV. This is still an active French military base, so visits to the facilities are limited. Check the website cited below to determine if tours are available for when you will be visiting.

Lille Citadel / Citadelle de Lille
Photo Source: Piocrr - Wikimedia Commons

<u>Lille Zoo / Zoo de Lille:</u> One of Lille's best attractions for children. It is a compact zoo of 8 acres which has roughly 100 species on display across seven geographical zones such as African Lands, American Lands, and more.

<u>Nature and Fitness Trails</u>: One of the most popular features of this large park are the long and varied trails. The trails are organized into "Loops" with the shortest being just 1km (about a half mile) and the longest, which is 5km. Each of the loops is organized into different themes such as a par course, a nature trail, a heritage trail, and more.

<u>Napoleon Bridge/Pont Napoleon:</u> Surrounding the park and the Citadel, is a river and set of canals. Several bridges span these canals and one of the more notable is the Napoleon Bridge. This is an ornate bridge that is a work of art in its own right. The bridge, originally constructed in 1812, has had a difficult history as it was destroyed both in WWI and WWII. It was rebuilt in

2014 to match previous design and standards. This is a wonderful photo opportunity which can easily be added in to exploring one of the park's attractive trails. The bridge crosses the canal along the eastern edge of the park and is easy to locate.

Porte Royale Entrance to the Citadel

<u>Hours & Fees:</u>

- The park is open during all daylight hours and there is no fee to enter.

- The Citadel is an active military base and is not generally open to casual visiting.

- The zoo's hours vary by the season but is always closed on Tuesday. During high season from early April to late September, it is open from 10am to 6pm. Entrance is free to holders of the Lille City Pass. Full rates are adult: 4.50€ and child rate of 2.50€. (These, and all fees cited in this guide are subject to change.)

The Napoleon Bridge / Pont Napoleon
One of many sights at the Citadel Park

Websites: **ParcDeLaCitadelle.Lille.fr**. This website includes information on all features of the park including trail information and admission information on the Citadel. Zoo.Lille.fr, focuses specifically on the zoo.

Getting Here: There is no nearby Metro stop here. If you wish to travel by bus, take Lines L1 or L5 to the "Champ de Mars" stop. From this bus stop, it is less than 10-minute walk to the Porte Royale gate of the citadel. Along the walk, is the entrance to the zoo. Near the bus stop, is a V'Lille bicycle rental station. If you are driving, there is a large parking area, so parking is generally easy to find. One caution, the park is the site of several large events so finding available parking at that time can be a challenge.

8: Attractions Near Lille

Not all of Lille's points of interest are in the city center. Lille's metropolitan area is spread out and several popular sights are in neighboring towns or suburbs. The good news is most of these can be reached by local transportation.

In several cases, the attractions are in towns which are great destinations in their own right. Good examples are the towns of Roubiax and Tourcoing. They are quiet, attractive towns to explore and easy to reach by local transportation. Consider combining a trip to one of the attractions such as the La Piscine Art and Industry Museum with casual exploring of the town's sights and cafes.

Some smaller museums are not listed here due to their limited hours. This includes the Resistance Museum in Bondues & the small Doll and Toy Museum in Wambrechies.

There are several opportunities to combine attractions due to their proximity to one another. A great example are the two textile museums in Roubaix. Another is in the suburb of Villeneuve-d'Ascq where several points of interest are close to the popular LaM Modern Art Museum.

> **Lille City Pass**
> Even though these attractions are outside of the city of Lille, most are included in the Lille City Pass.

Map #	Name	Town	Travel Time	Public Transport
\multicolumn{5}{c}{**Nearby Points of Interest Outlined in this Chapter**}
\multicolumn{5}{c}{Travel Time is estimated from central Lille}
\multicolumn{5}{c}{Map #s are from the map on the next page.}

Map #	Name	Town	Travel Time	Public Transport
1	La Piscine Art & Industry Museum	Roubaix	25 min	Metro + Bus
2	Textile Mfg. Museum		30+ min	
3	Villa Cavrois	Croix	18 min	No
4	LaM Modern Art	Villeneuve-d'Ascq	15+ min	Bus
5	Open Air Museum		20 min	No
7	Fort Seclin	Seclin	25 min	Bus

Using one of the popular Lille apps will help greatly in planning your day and how you travel to these towns and attractions. Suggest using one of the following for these trips:

- City Pass Lille Métropole
- Lille Travel Guide
- Lille Metro & Tram Map

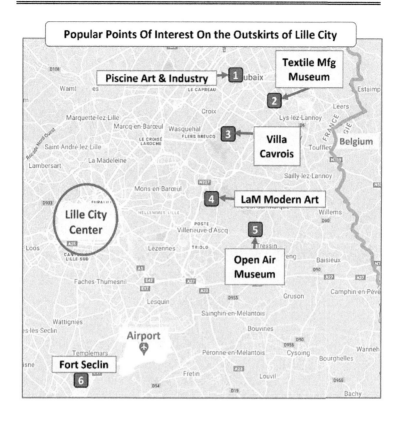

Popular Points Of Interest On the Outskirts of Lille City

1 - Piscine Art & Industry Museum / La Piscine Musée d'Art et d'Industrie:

Description: The French term "La Piscine" means swimming pool and this is an apt description for the unique setting of this museum. This area has a long history of fabric manufacturing. The museum focuses on the art and technology behind textiles and ceramics with an additional sizeable collection of painting and sculptures.

La Piscine - a Museum of Arts & Industry with an Art Deco Swimming Pool as its centerpiece.

In 2000, a large permanent collection of textiles was placed into a building which had previously been an ornate indoor swimming pool. Today, the pool still exists, although very shallow, and is framed by many works of art. Among the interesting exhibit settings are the old shower stalls which are now display cases and alcoves.

Entry Fees: Free, if you hold a Lille City Pass. Normal adult rate is 9 €. Rates may be higher when special, temporary exhibits are occurring.

Hours: Closed on Mondays. On weekends, it is only open in the afternoon and early evening from 1pm to 6pm. Weekdays, Tue to Fri, it is open from 11am to 6pm.

Website: **Roubaix-Lapiscine.com**

Where Located & What is Nearby: Roubaix is a pleasant town very close to the border to Belgium. The central Grand Place is a good place to begin explorations and there are many cafes and shops here. If you travel here by Metro, it is a pleasant walk to the museum which is tucked back from a main thoroughfare.

Getting Here: The address is 23, rue de l'Expérance, Roubaix.

The local metro is the best mode of transportation from Lille and there are two stations to select from. First option is to take the Metro line #2 to the Roubaix Grand Place station. From there, it is a 6-to-9-minute walk to the museum. A V'Lille bicycle rental station is also available at the metro/train station.

> View Both Textile Oriented Museums
> Consider, when visiting Roubaix, a visit to both the La Piscine and the Textile Manufacturing Museum. Together, they provide a comprehensive view of the textile industry.

An alternative is to take the metro to the Eurotéléport station in Roubaix and take the bus or walk 10+ minutes to the museum. While this is a longer walk to La Piscine, it has the two advantages of the station being in an appealing section of town and it is between La Piscine and the Textile Manufacturing Museum (description follows). This makes visiting the two museums in one day easy to do.

2 - Textile Manufacturing Museum / La Manufacture de Roubaix

Description: This is one of two museums in Roubaix largely devoted to textiles. While the above cited La Piscine Museum focuses more on the art of fabric and design, this museum is devoted to the technology and production techniques of textiles. A highlight of this manufacturing museum is a broad array of equipment and tools crafted to help in the manufacturing of differing fabrics.

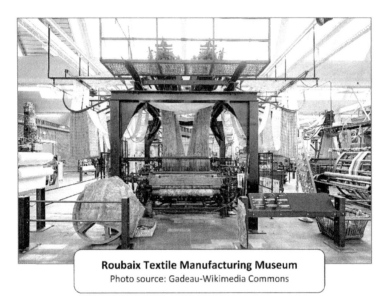

Roubaix Textile Manufacturing Museum
Photo source: Gadeau-Wikimedia Commons

When visiting this museum, guided tours are available, typically around 2, 3, and 4pm. These are highly recommended as there is quite an array of complex equipment here and a skilled guide can greatly increase your understanding of the sights before you.

Entry Fees: Normal adult rate is 6€. If you have a Lille City Pass, there is no fee to enter.

Hours: Closed on Mondays. Open 2pm to 6pm Tuesday to Sunday. It is not open in the morning except for prearranged group tours. Guided tours are available and advised, so check the schedule when you arrive.

Website: LaManufacture-Roubaix.com

<u>Where Located & What is Nearby</u>: The area around the museum has little to offer in the way of dining or shopping. This makes sense given the industrial nature and history of this neighborhood. Consider heading back to Eurotéléport Metro station which is quite active for any exploring you may want to do.

<u>Getting Here</u>: The address is 29, avenue Julien Lagache, Roubaix.

This museum sits away from central Roubaix and walking to it from the train or metro station is not recommended. If you are not driving, take the Metro to Eurotéléport station and bus #3 to the Leers La Plaine stop.

3 - Villa Cavrois / La Villa Cavrois:

<u>Description:</u> Of the seven attractions outlined in this chapter, the Villa Cavrois is the most subdued. A visit to this large villa, which is officially labeled as an historic monument, consists of a tour of an architectural masterpiece and grounds. It is not a museum in the purest sense, rather it is a visit to an expansive and unique mansion. The villa was built in 1932 to house Paul Cavrois and his family, a former owner of upscale manufacturing in Roubaix.

This large villa of over 30,000 sq feet (2,800 sq meters) was built by architect Mallet-Stevens in a modernistic style. To many, this building and the furnishings are reminiscent of Frank Lloyd Wright in North America. Every aspect of the design, including all of the furniture, was designed by the architect.

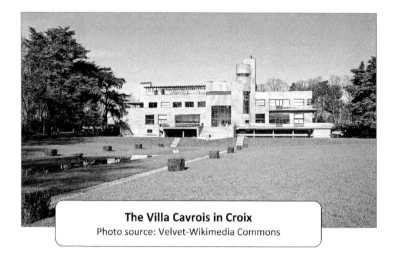

The Villa Cavrois in Croix
Photo source: Velvet-Wikimedia Commons

Self-guided tours are available, and visitors are provided with guidebooks which are available in English and several other languages. There is a gift shop and restrooms on site.

Entry Fees: Free if you have a Lille City Pass. Normal adult rate is 11€. Combination, discounted passes which include this and the two textile museums in Roubaix.

Hours: Closed on Mondays. Open 10am to 6pm Tuesday to Sunday.

Website: **Villa-Cavrois.fr**

Where Located & What is Nearby: The monument is near the village of Croix which is between Lille and Roubaix. There is, unfortunately, very little else in the immediate area. Near the metro stop are a few fast-food restaurants and little else.

Getting Here: The address is 60 Avenue Kennedy, Croix

This museum is in a residential area and easy to miss as it gives the appearance from the road of being another house in the neighborhood. The best way to travel here is by car, but note that parking spaces are limited. If you wish to use public transportation, take the light rail to the Villa Cravois station. From there, it is a 12-15+ minute walk along quiet, residential streets.

The Villeneuve-d'Ascq Area:

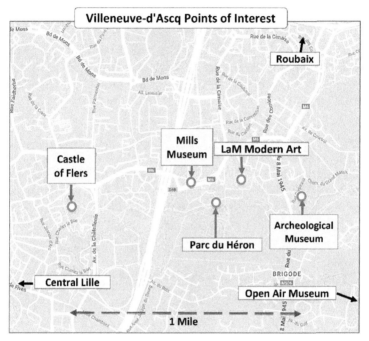

The following descriptions outline the popular LaM Modern Art Museum and the Open-Air Museum, both of which are in the Villeneuve-d'Ascq area. This area is just a short distance east of central Lille and south of Roubaix.

There is far more here than just these two museums and visitors could easily spend a full day or more exploring the sights of this relaxed area. Neighboring attractions, all of which are near each other but not necessarily in walking distance, include:

Parc du Héron: A 270-acre park and greenspace with numerous trails and a lake and river to explore. It is immediately next to the LaM Modern Art Museum making it easy to visit both.

Mills Museum / Musée des Moulins: Think of windmills and the work these important and attractive structures did and this is what you will find here. Several restored windmills and a museum are in this open area. It is close to the LaM Modern Art Museum and within walking distance.

Archeological Museum / Musée d'Archéologie Asnapio: A after a 10-minute walk east off the LaM Museum, there is a small archeology museum which presents how life was in Neolithic and Paleolithic times. For details, check out the website at: Asnapio.Villeneuvedascq.fr.

Castle of Flers / Château de Flers: Slightly west of the Mills Museum and the LaM Modern Art Museum is the Castle of Flers. This 17th century Flemish castle provides tours of the castle and grounds. The town's tourist office is located here which can be helpful. A drive from here to the LaM and other attractions is warranted as it is a 20+ minute walk.

4 - LaM Modern Art Museum / Lille Métropole Musée d'art Moderne:

Description: This is a multi-faceted experience with a large museum, sculpture park, and adjoining nature park. The museum, which focuses on modern and contemporary art, houses over 7,000 items. Works include many of the world's top contemporary artists such as Joan Miro, Picasso, Alexander Calder, and Modigliani.

This museum is considered to be the only one in all of Europe to house all schools of 20th and 21st century art with the many galleries displaying brut art, contemporary, and modern art.

The LaM Modern Art Museum
Adjacent to a large park, sculpture garden, and greenspace.
Photo source: Google Earth

This is a large facility, spread over many galleries. Plan on spending a minimum of two hours here. The facility also includes a gift shop, restaurant, and library.

In addition to the museum, several works are placed into something of a sculpture park set into a section of the adjoining nature park. This provides an enjoyable game to explore the park's trails and discover the works placed here.

Entry Fees: Normal adult rate is 7€. If you have a Lille City Pass, there is no entry fee.

Hours: Closed on Mondays. Open Tuesday through Sunday from 10am to 6pm.

Website: **Musee-lam.fr**

Where Located & What is Nearby: The museum and sculpture park is adjacent to a large park with many trails. There are also several other attractions nearby. See the section in this chapter just before the description of the LaM Museum for a listing of nearby sights. Also adjacent to the museum are two enjoyable restaurants. Consider either sitting outside in the area provided or pick up a lunch to take into the park.

Getting Here: The address is 1 All du Musée, Villeneuve-d'Ascq.

The best way to reach this museum and area is either to drive or take the local bus. There is no Metro or Light Rail stop nearby. To travel

Find works such as this one by Picasso in the LaM Sculpture Garden
Photo source: Michiel1972-Wikimedia Commons

by bus, take either route 32 or L6 to the LAM stop. The Ilivia.fr website and app are good methods for determining how best to travel the area and which routes to take.

5 - Open Air Museum / Musée de Plein Air:

Description: Take a step back in time and stroll through a reconstructed village and farm. Over the years, several historic structures were saved from demolition and moved here.

There are over twenty different types of buildings dating from the 17th century to early 19th century. They include homes, workshops, and old stores. In addition, there are orchards and gardens reconstructed to match earlier times. A highlight during prime season is to watch skilled craftspeople in period costume present woodworking, weaving, and more.

A tavern which serves cuisine from the period is on site and is a great place to relax.

Open Air Museum & Historic Village
Photo source: Pierre Leclercq-Wikimedia Commons

<u>Entry Fees:</u> Normal adult rate is 5€ or 15 Euro for a family. This pass covers several parks throughout the Lille area.

<u>Hours:</u> Seasonal from mid-April to late October. Hours vary by the season, so checking the website for hours when you will be there is advised. During the prime months of June through August, it is open every day starting at 10am and closes at 6pm or 7pm depending on the day. Unlike most attractions in the area, this location is open on Monday.

<u>Website:</u> **enm.LilleMetropole.fr/parcs/Musee-de-Plein-Air**

<u>Where Located & What is Nearby:</u> This open-air museum is in a rural setting and, aside from a nearby pet cemetery which can be interesting in its own way, there is little close by.

<u>Getting Here:</u> The address is 143 Rue Colbert, Villeneuve-d'Ascq.

Given the rural location, traveling by car is suggested. Bus travel can be done but is not advised as the closest stop is at least a 15-minute walk from the Open-Air Museum.

6 - Fort Seclin / Fort de Seclin:

Fort Seclin - WW1 & WWII Fortification
Photo source: Heraldix-Wikimedia Commons

Description: Also known as Fort Duhoux. Coming here is an excellent way to experience what fortifications and defense in the area was like in the late 19th century and early 20th century. Fort Seclin is one of several forts which were established after the Franco-Prussian War. Later, it had a limited role in WWI and no significant action in WWII.

The fort is built in a trapezoidal shape, a design common for the era. Around forty pieces of artillery were placed around the fort and, at its most active, housed nearly 800 men.

Today, much of the fort and surrounding grounds are open to explore and guided tours are available. It is a private museum and was opened in 2003 by the owners. Inside the fort and its buildings, is a museum which focuses on armaments common through the era, with a focus on WWI and the France-Prussian War.

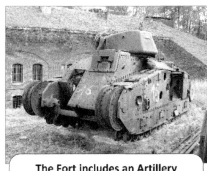

The Fort Includes an Artillery Museum
Photo source: The Shadock-Wikimedia Commons

Entry Fees: Normal adult rate is 6€ or 4€ for 8–15-year-olds. Free to children under 8. Private group tours may be booked in advance for 50€.

Hours: Closed on Sunday. Monday, only open in the afternoon from 2pm to 5:30pm. Tuesday to Saturday, open from 9am to 12:30pm, then reopens from 2pm to 5:30pm. Saturday, morning only from 9am to 12:30pm.

Website: FortSeclin.com

Where Located & What is Nearby: The fort is due south of central Lille by 10 miles and about a mile from the airport. The closest facilities are in an area of strip malls and auto dealers a short distance to the west. No other attractions are nearby.

Getting Here: The address is Chem du Fort, Seclin.

While the museum is close to the Lille airport, it is not convenient to any public transportation. Cars are needed to visit this site.

9: Shopping in Central Lille

The good news in central Lille is you don't have to go far to find just about everything you might want for shopping, browsing, and dining. If you consider the Grand Place as the epicenter of historic Lille and its shopping opportunities, all but one of the recommended shopping areas in this guide are within a 10-minute walk.

Planning Note: Many shops are closed on Sunday.

When visiting any city, shopping destinations generally fall into four broad categories: (a) city streets and plazas with a variety of stores and restaurants, (b) local markets and farmers markets which focus on cuisine and crafts, (c) shopping centers which generally cater to local shopping and not tourism, and (d) stand-alone stores away from active shopping areas which are special in their own right, such as several museum shops which deserve their own special mention. Lille has all of these near the center of town.

There are 6 suggested shopping areas, malls, and local markets in Lille to explore.

Grand Place / Place du Général de Gaulle: With this large and iconic plaza being such a center for tourism and activities, it is no surprise that it is a good place to shop, not only for the expected tourist gifts, but there are several unique destinations here as well:

- **Old Stock Exchange / Le Vielle Bourse:** During the summer months, a book exchange is held Tuesday through Sunday. You may also find chess games going on. It is a great place to pick up a treasured book or comic.

- **Furet du Nord:** A huge, 8-floor, bookstore adjacent to the Grand Place. It is considered to be one of the best bookstores in northern France.

- **Comptoir des Monnaies:** Interested in historic coins and jewelry? Check out this shop and, who knows, you might just find that perfect gift for the coin collector in your life.

- **Souvenirs Lille:** As the title indicates, this store, which is on the Grand Place, carries a good variety of local souvenirs and regional items.

- **Rue Esquermoise:** There are several lanes leading off from the Grand Place which have many specialty stores. One of the best is Rue Esquermoise which heads northwest from the plaza. Along here are numerous gift shops, fashion boutiques, candles, and cosmetic shops.

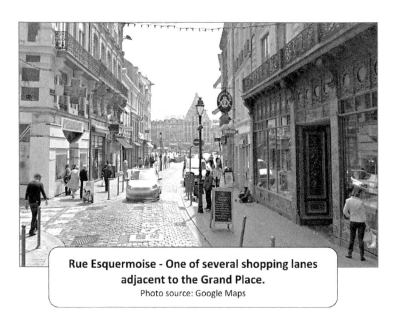

Rue Esquermoise - One of several shopping lanes adjacent to the Grand Place.
Photo source: Google Maps

Place Rihour: In all probability, after spending only a short while in Lille, you will have been to or through this busy square which is close to the Grand Place at least once. Not only is this the location of Lille's Tourist Office, but it is also the location of a busy Metro stop, the closest Metro station to the Grand Place.

Lille's Office de Tourisme is a good place to find local souvenirs.
Photo source: Lille Tourism

One great aspect of Place Rihour are the many restaurants here which includes cafes, bistros, and upscale dining. For shopping, the number of stores here is not large, but there are some notable shopping spots here including:

- **Printemps:** This is an upscale department store chain in France, along the lines of the Galleries Lafayette. This location of Printemps, next to the Tourist Office, is a close copy of the central Paris site so, if you are seeking quality clothing or cosmetics, this is the place to go.

- **Tourist Office / Office de Tourisme:** If you are seeking gifts which are specific to Lille, the Tourist Office located on Place Rihour is a good place to start.

- **Christmas Market / Village de Noël:** This plaza is one of the top destinations each Christmas season when the multi-location Lille Christmas Market is in place. Head to Place Rihour to find numerous stalls selling local crafts and treats.

Euralille Shopping Center / Westfield Euralille: If you arrived in Lille by train at the Gare Lille Europe, you will probably walk right by this huge and modern shopping center. It is big enough to warrant even having an app to help you navigate you though the multi-story mall.

The massive Euralille Center sits between Lille's two train stations.
Photo source: Velvet - Wikimedia Commons

There are over 130 stores here, with most stores matching what you would want in a typical large, urban shopping mall that is designed to service the needs of residents. In addition to clothing, cosmetics, and top European brand shops, there is also a large Carrefour market. There are many food outlets here in addition to stores. Most dining options lean toward casual fare.

The Euralille Mall is closed on Sunday.

To view all that this large mall has to offer, check out the website at: Fr.Westfield.com/Euralille.

Other Shopping Centers in Lille:

The Euralille is not the only sizeable shopping center in central Lille. There are two other malls near the heart of town which are worth exploring, although neither is as large or popular as the Euralille Center.

- **Tanneurs Shopping Center / Centre Commercial Les Tanneurs:** This mall is unusual in that it is tucked away, and you pretty much have to know it is there to find it. It sits two blocks southeast from Place Rihour and the Grand Place.

  One of the leading streets where you can find the mall is on Rue des Tanneurs. Two highlights of this mall are the large food court and a very large Monoprix grocery store.

  The website for this mall is: **www.LesTanneurs.com**

- **Lillenium / Centre Commercial Lillenium:** This mall may be larger than the Euralille with over 100 stores and restaurants.

  It is a popular destination for area residents but, for visitors, it presents the challenge of not being directly in the heart of town. It lies just outside of the main highway circle and is best reached by bus. Walking to this mall is not advised. To view details on this modern mall, check out **www.Lillenium-Lille.com**

  All malls in Lille are closed on Sunday.

Old Town Lille / Le Vieux-Lille: Slightly northwest of the Grande Place, is an area of narrow, meandering, streets and many prominent buildings such as Comtesse Hospice and Notre-Dame Cathedral (Notre-Dame-de-la-Trielle Cathedral). Throughout this area are several shops and cafés which are largely oriented to fill the needs of residents. It is a perfect area to explore local patisseries, bookshops, and clothing boutiques and shop as the locals do.

The area around the cathedral is noted for its many Leather Goods shops such as the Paul Marius Boutique shown here.

Among the many boutiques which line the streets here are several leather goods shops. Check out stores such as Hermès, Louis Vuitton, Paul Marius, Repetto, and many others for the best in shoes, boots, and handbags. This area of town is noted for its specialty leather goods.

A good starting point for explorations here is Rue Basse, a lane which runs east-west and just below the cathedral. From here, head northeast to where the street changes its name to Rue des Chats Bossus. All along the way, you will find great browsing and dining opportunities.

If you enjoy open air markets, check out the "Marché du Vieux-Lille" or Old Lille Market. Located at the small Place du Concert a short distance north of central Old Town, this market is open on Wednesday, Friday, and Sunday from 7am to 2pm. You will find an assortment of baked items, textiles, and some fresh produce.

Wazemmes Market / Les Halles de Wazemmes: Lille has several markets which roughly fall into the category of "farmers and crafts markets."

In Lille, the Wazemmes market is by far the largest and most popular of these "Marchés." Hundreds of stalls and booths may be found here when the market is at its busiest. Most of the stalls in the covered area are permanent. It is a wonderful way to obtain a broad sampling of the best in area meats, poultry, dessert items, and even fabrics.

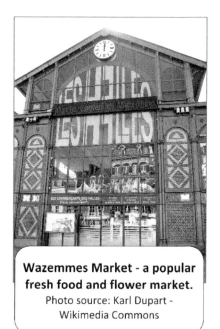

Wazemmes Market - a popular fresh food and flower market.
Photo source: Karl Dupart - Wikimedia Commons

Hours: The market is open every day except Monday, but the best times to visit are on Tuesday, Thursday, and Sunday from 7am to 7pm when both the indoor/covered market and outdoor stalls are active. The covered market is open every Tuesday to Saturday from 8am to 8pm, but there is less activity and fewer stalls open at this time.

Location: This market is southwest from the Grand Place and can be a bit of a walk from the historic area so, for most of us, taking the Metro can be the best way to travel here. The Gambetta Metro stop is only a 4-minute walk away. There is also a Metro stop with the name of Wazemmes, but it is further away.

10: Area Cuisine & Dining

When looking for dining locales and dishes which are representative of the area,[12] Lille offers a variety of Flemish and French dishes. Often, dishes providing a unique blend of the two regions will be found.

Some popular dishes for the area include:

<u>Moules-Frites:</u> A Flemish standard found throughout this area of France and much of Belgium. With the coast nearby, this is a local dish to find. It is a mix of local fries with one or more small pots of area mussels.

<u>Raclette:</u> Another delight for cheese lovers. In essence, this dish is a grilled cheese wheel

Try the area specialty of "Moules-Frites" (Mussels and Fries) while in LIlle.

---

[12] Lillois Fare: You will often find the term "Lillois" used when describing the area's cuisine. The dishes listed here are all popular to Lille, but may not be limited to this area.

served with another layer of melted cheese and bread or chips.

<u>Le Welsh</u>: A popular dish found in many area restaurants. Despite the name, it has nothing to do with Wales. It is a cheese-lovers delight with bread, ham, and some vegetables under a bed of melted cheese. The ingredients hidden under the layer of cheese can vary by the restaurant.

<u>Carbonnade Flamande</u>: A hefty regional stew with a mix of beef chunks in dark beer and gravy. It is typically flavored with brown sugar and mustard. Come hungry.

<u>Merveilleux</u>: The perfect desert for chocolate aficionados. Picture a delightful mound of meringue topped with whipped cream and grated chocolate.

If you love Chocolate, try the "Merveilleux" in LIlle.
Photo Source: Eeicing - Wikimedia Commons

<u>Local Cheeses</u>: Throughout France, you will find cheeses which are unique to the region and the Nord region of France is no exception. When dining or visiting a specialty market such as Wazemmes, look for such delights as (and not limited to):

- <u>Aumoniè de l'Ecaillon</u> – a soft cheese with the scent of fresh hay and dried fruit. It is often filled with local fruit or jelly.

- <u>Mimolette</u>: Served as a ball which can be up to 6-inches across. It is medium in hardness and orange in color with a fruity scent.

- <u>Bergues</u>: A medium-soft cheese that comes from the Dunkirk area. Made from cow's milk, it is a pleasant and smooth cheese which is perfect on a salad.

Some Restaurants & Bistros to Consider:

With hundreds of restaurants, bistros, and nightclubs in central Lille, you don't have to go far to find food and snack options to match your preference. To help guide you in your search, following is a list of restaurants which serve one or more of the area's specialty dishes. This list is a composite of well-rated locales from a variety of sources and personal experiences.

Old Town Lille has many spots to sit outside and dine such as the Estaminet Au Vieux De La Vieille **on Place aux Oignons.**

Dining preferences can and do vary wildly by every individual and it is advised to use one of the many highly detailed and up-to-date reference sites such as Trip Advisor. These websites can answer every question you may have and, in many cases, allow you to make reservations online.

Four sections of Lille are outlined here. In each of the areas depicted on the map on the previous page, there is a great mix of options ranging from fast food, national chains, and specialty restaurants.

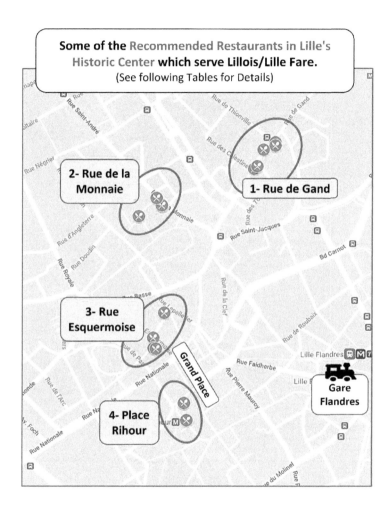

Some of the Recommended Restaurants in Lille's **Historic Center which serve Lillois/Lille Fare.**
(See following Tables for Details)

1. Rue de Gand: A northern section of Lille's Old Town and roughly an 8-to-10-minute walk north from the Grand Place. This is an area noted for the many Flemish styled buildings, quaint homes, and popular bistros. The street, "Rue de Gand," is an extension of the long Place Louise de Bettignies.

101

The entire area is filled with eating establishments many of which reflect other cultures such as Asian cuisine.

1 - Suggested Dining Spots Near Rue de Gand		
(All selected dining spots provide area/Lille cuisine)		
Restaurant	**Address**	**Rating**
A Taaable	62 Rue de Gand — 4 stars Small French restaurant, fairly formal. Offers a mix of Flemish & French dishes. www.ATaaableRestaurant.fr.	
Comptoir 44	44 Rue de Gand — 4.5 stars Upscale bistro with inviting atmosphere. www.Comptoir44-Lille.fr	
Le Bistrot Lillois	40 Rue de Gand — 4 stars Casual atmosphere with focus on local dishes. Very popular and can fill up quickly.	
La Crêperie de Lille	64 Rue de Gand — 4.5 stars As the name says, come for the crepes. Moderately priced with informal atmosphere. www.Creperie-Lille.fr	
Estaminet Du Welsh	45 Rue de Gand — 4.5 stars Menu is focused to local cuisine. Check out their Le Welsh. Very casual setting. www.WellWelsh.com	
La Terrasse des Remparts	92 Rue de Gand — 5 stars Highly rated. A bit further north than other establishments cited here. Great outdoor	

1 - Suggested Dining Spots Near Rue de Gand		
(All selected dining spots provide area/Lille cuisine)		
Restaurant	**Address**	**Rating**
	courtyard in a building which towers over the area. Fairly formal and one of the more expensive listed here. www.LilleRemparts.fr	

2. **Rue de la Monnaie:** Slightly north of the cathedral is the popular dining area along Rue de la Monnaie. This is a long street which changes names several times as it wraps around the cathedral and connects with Rue Basse.

There are some notable alleys or side streets which lead to hidden gems for dining such as Rue de Pétérinck which leads to Place aux Oignons. This area is easily reached on foot from the Grand Place by heading north for 7 to 10 minutes through the pleasant maze which is Old Town Lille.

In addition to restaurants which serve local cuisine, such as those highlighted in the following table, you will find several popular pizza and Italian restaurants as well.

2 - Suggested Dining Spots Near Rue de la Monnaie		
Restaurant	**Address**	**Rating**
Estaminet Au Vieu De La Vielle	2 Rue des Vieux Murs Tucked away on the nearly hidden Place aux Oignons, this is one of the most popular French restaurants in central Lille with a focus on local dishes. Cozy interior and great outdoor seating area. www.EstaminetLille.fr.	4 stars

2 - Suggested Dining Spots Near Rue de la Monnaie		
Restaurant	**Address**	**Rating**
L'Assiette du Marché	61 Rue de la Monnaie 4 stars A bit upscale and more formal than many of the nearby establishments. A broad menu with many local and traditional French dishes. www.AssietteDuMarche.com	
Le Barbier qui fume Vieux Lille	69 Rue de la Monnaie 4.5 stars Another popular spot along this active street. Enjoyable outdoor dining. Traditional French menu at moderate prices www.LeBarbierQuiFume.fr	
La Petite Table	59 Rue de la Monnaie 4 stars Small, thus the name "petite," restaurant which would be easy to miss if you weren't looking for it. Casual atmosphere with a limited number of tables. Try their Le Welsh. www.LaPetiteTable-VieuxLille.com	

3. **Rue Esquermoise**: Adjacent to the Grand Place's northern side is Rue Esquermoise, an enjoyable street and area for both dining and shopping. The busy street heads north for several blocks until it morphs into Rue Royale which is also a good area to browse.

Several notable dining establishments that serve local and French cuisine may be found along here. Note that several of the better establishments here are not directly on Rue Esquermoise, but may be off on one of the small side streets which take off from here.

3 - Suggested Dining near Rue Esquermoise

Restaurant	Address	Rating
Crêperie Beaurepaire	1 Rue Saint-Etienne 4 stars This restaurant is a hidden gem, tucked away on a narrow lane which connects Rue Esquermoise to Rue de Pas. A well-rated creperie in a cozy atmosphere and little courtyard to enjoy local fare. www.CreperieBeauRepaire.com.	
Le Barbue d'Anvers	1 Rue Saint-Etienne 4 stars Casual, tavern-like, establishment in the same building on Rue Saint-Etienne as the above cited Crêperie Beaurepaire. www.BarbueDAnvers.fr	
La Petite Cour	1 Rue du Cour Saint-Etienne 4 stars This small bistro is also tucked away on Saint-Etienne. Due to its popularity, it can be very crowded. A broad menu serving local, French, and Flemish dishes. Try dining in their courtyard in good weather. www.LaPetiteCour-Lille.fr	
Pâtisserie Méert	25 Rue Esquermoise 4.5 stars If you are seeking wonderful desserts in an elegant atmosphere, look no further. Moderately priced with informal atmosphere. Try their Merveilleux, or De Gaulle's vanilla waffles. www.Meert.fr	

4. **Place Rihour**: The small plaza, Place Rihour, which sits just one block southwest from the Grand Place, is another section of town where a few quality restaurants serving regional dishes may be found. It is very easy to reach as the Metro stops here.

   Many of the establishments here lean more toward casual such as bars or sandwich shops, but you will find a small number of places (cited in the table below) which can match many of those in the areas outlined earlier in this chapter.

   Place Rihour is also the location of the Tourist office, the Printemps department store, and even a specialty restaurant serving African cuisine. Most of the restaurants here are on Pl Rihour, the short street which connects Place Rihour with the Grand Place.

1 - Suggested Dining Spots Near Place Rihour		
Restaurant	**Address**	**Rating**
Brasserie La Chicorée	51 Pl Rihour 3.5 stars Casual, inviting, atmosphere, and a great place to find local dishes such as Moules-Frites. **www.Brasserie-LaChicoree.fr.**	
Café Peacock	14 Pl Rihour 4 stars A good mixture of local café with cocktail bar. Their specialty is the Peacock Cocktail. **www.Cafe-Peacock.fr**	
Révelle	35 bis Pl Rihour 4 stars This restaurant is directly on Place Rihour, immediately next to the Metro entrance. A great spot for breakfast or brunch.	

11: Day Trips by Train Near Lille

Exploring the towns, battlefields, and coastal areas in the Nord Department of France around Lille is fun and there are many to choose from. A sampling of the more popular day trip opportunities is described in this chapter. Each of these four destinations fit the criteria of (a) being within 90 minutes by train each way from Lille, and (b) offer a variety of sights which can

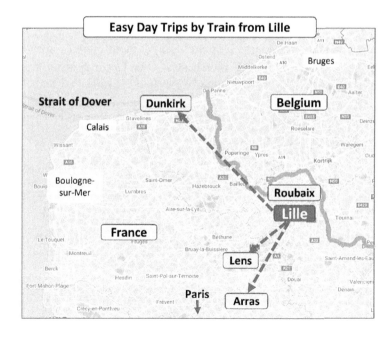

Consider a Guided Tour

In addition to the self-guided trips outlined here, consider one of the many guided group tours which depart out of Lille, such as one of the Battlefield Tours.

Resources for these tours include (and not limited to):

- Lille Tourist Office
- Viator.com / TripAdvisor.com
- GetYourGuide.com
- Expedia.com

---

easily be reached on foot or local transportation from the train station. Beyond the four cited below, there are several other destinations, but are not listed due to their similarity to the four outlined here.

In addition, many battlefields and monuments, most of which are from WWI, are often best reached by car or group tour and do not fit the criteria of easily reached via train.

Day Trip Destinations near Lille		
(Reachable by train in under 90 minutes)		
Destination	**Nature of Destination**	**Train Travel Time**
Arras	Beautiful mid-sized town with scenic grand plazas similar to Lille.	30 to 45 minutes
Dunkirk	Attractive port city and locale of several major battlefields.	1 hr 10 min

Day Trip Destinations near Lille		
(Reachable by train in under 90 minutes)		
Destination	**Nature of Destination**	**Train Travel Time**
Lens	Home to the notable extension of Paris's Louvre-Lens Museum.	40+ min
Roubaix or Tourcoing	The closest to Lille of the destinations outlined here. Attractive towns with several museums.	15+ min
Check rome2Rio.com for train and bus schedules You may also purchase tickets from this and similar websites.		

Arras, France:

In many ways, Arras feels like a scaled-down version of Lille. This small city of 42,000 is a visual delight with abundant Flemish architecture. Located less than an hour south of Lille, it is easy to reach and explore once you are there.

In Arras, you have a Grand Place just as in Lille and another notable plaza the Heroes Square (Place des Héros). With all of the beautiful buildings bordering these large squares, it is hard to believe that over two-thirds of the town was destroyed during WWI and significant action occurred here in WWII. As a result of the rebuilding, the buildings around the central squares can fool you somewhat as they are not as old as their design would cause you to think. Most were rebuilt after the wars.

Place des Héros & Arras Belfry

Start your explorations at Heroes Square. This impressive plaza houses the city's tourist office, the Hôtel de Ville, and the tall belfry which towers over the town. This square and adjoining structures have been designated a World Heritage Site.

Popular in town sights include the cathedral built in the 18th century and a large Beaux-Arts Museum which is housed in a former Abbey. On the outskirts of town, are notable military sites (not walkable) including an impressive citadel and an impressive war memorial in Vimy honoring the fallen Canadian soldiers.

Traveling to Arras: Take a train from the Lille Flandres station directly to Arras. There are numerous departures daily, so it is generally easy to fit one into your preferred schedule. Direct departures typically take 35 to 40 minutes. Take care as some departures require a change in the town of Lens and this can more than double travel time. However, this also provides the ability to stop over in Lens and view the expansive art museum there.

The Arras train station is adjacent to an attractive plaza. From there, it is less than a 10-minute walk to the heart of town. Consider heading to Heroes Square to begin your explorations. Have a map or map app with you as there is no direct route to the plaza.

> If you are in Arras during **Christmas,** you will find one of the region's largest Christmas markets.

If you prefer, local buses can take you into the center of town or even out to the citadel. A map of their route is posted at the Gare/train station.

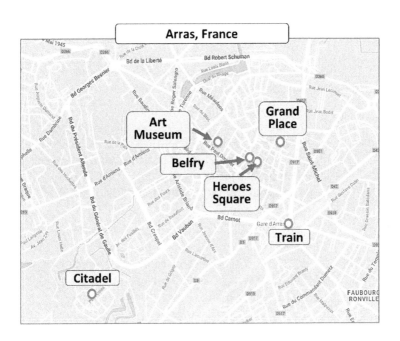

Arras Highlights:

- Heroes Square / Place des Héros: This square and adjoining buildings have been designated as a World Heritage Site. There are many wonderful photo opportunities here. In addition to the many shops and cafes, the Arras Tourist Office and the Hôtel de Ville are located on the square.

- Arras Belfry / Le Beffroi d'Arras: Towering 246 feet (75 meters) over Heroes Square is the impressive Belfry of Arras. It had been destroyed in WWI and was rebuilt in 1931. Visitors may purchase tickets to travel to the top. The trip up includes a mix of elevator and stairs and is not advised for individuals who are mobility impaired.

- Grand Place/The Grand Place: A large open square which is ringed by attractive Flemish-style buildings. Unlike Lille where the Grand Place is the central point of the city, the above cited Heroes Square is the primary spot in Arras. There are numerous shops, cafes, and restaurants around the four sides of this square.

- Beaux-Arts Museum /Musée des Beaux-Arts: A fascinating aspect of this prominent art museum is the building it sits in, the "Abbey of St. Vaast." The museum's collection includes many Flemish and Dutch masters in addition to prehistoric artifacts and sculptures. It is located at 22 Rue Paul Doumer which is a 5-minute walk northwest from Heroes Square.

- The Citadel of Arras:/Citadelle d'Arras: This historical landmark is a large complex of buildings in a 17th century fortification. The fortification was built in a star shape and much of the early walls are still intact. It includes a chapel, small museum, and expansive walking paths. This fort is not within easy walking distance of central Arras, but city buses are available.

<u>Arras Website:</u> The Arras Tourist Office has a comprehensive website which details current events and the town's attractions: www.Arras-France.com.

Dunkirk / Dunkerque:

Dunkirk is a plesant coastal town to explore.
(Hôtel de Ville towering over the town and harbor)
Photo source: Velvet-Wikimedia Commons

This town of nearly ninety thousand people shares little in common with Lille. It is a large beach and harbor town with a bit of an industrial feel. It is not a city filled with historic Flemish buildings but does provide a pleasant laid-back feel of a beach town. It has France's third largest harbor with only Le Havre and Marseille beating it in size.

This is a destination city for many families from areas of Europe and England. It's lengthy, sandy beaches lined with hotels are very inviting and make for a great vacation area. The area is often called the Opal Coast. This coastline spans 75 miles with great expanses of pristine beaches, often lined with white cliffs.

Within the central area of town there is a pleasant mix of old and new. The Dunkirk Belfry which shares a plaza with the historic Saint-Éloi Catholic Church makes for an excellent starting point. The Tourist Office is on the ground floor of the Belfry. Use this facility to obtain detailed information and maps on the town, its attractions and available tours.

Traveling to Dunkirk: If you travel by train, most trips from Lille will take just slightly over one hour and will depart from the Lille Flandres station. Trains depart frequently throughout the day so finding one to fit your preference should be easy. Take care to pick a direct train as some trains will cause you to change midway, adding time to your trip.

The Dunkirk train station is adjacent to an attractive plaza. It is a level walk along moderately busy streets into the heart of town or to the marina area. Walking time into the center of town will be around ten minutes. Do not attempt to walk to the beach as this can take well over thirty minutes.

> Travel FREE on most bus routes in central Dunkirk.

Dunkirk has a comprehensive bus system and, if you wish to travel to the shore or any of the war memorials on the edge of town, buses are suggested. Covered bus terminals, with maps of the system, are next to the train station. Details on bus routes in Dunkirk may be found at www.DKBus.com.

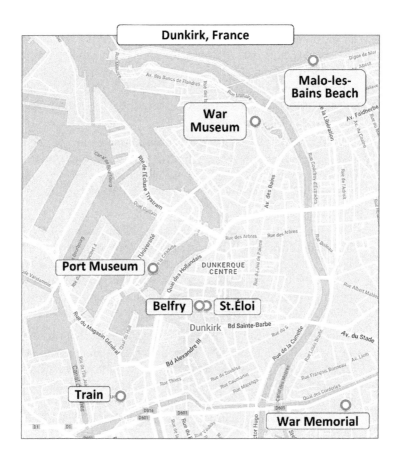

Dunkirk Highlights: There are numerous points of interest in and near Dunkirk ranging from local beaches to an aquarium, several museums, and many war memorials. Listed below are several of the more popular destinations which represent a fair cross-section of all this town and area have to offer. Consider, when arriving in Dunkirk, heading directly to the Tourist Office located in the Saint-Éloi Belfry. This office can provide you with a detailed attractions map.

- Saint-Éloi Belfry / Le Beffroi de Saint-Éloi: Sitting in the center of town is an attractive bell tower which was built in the 15th century and rises 190 feet (58 meters). It is located next to the historic Saint-Éloi Catholic Church. You may visit the upper portions of the belfry where there is a viewing platform. This is an excellent spot to view the city, harbor area, and some of the coastline.

   To reach the top, there is a combination of elevator and stairs. The 65 stairs can be limiting to some individuals. There is a fee for adults of five Euro to visit the top. The website for this tower is **www.Beffroi-Dunkerque.fr.**

- Saint-Éloi Catholic Church /Église Catholique Saint-Éloi: A Roman Catholic Church which carries the nickname of "Cathedral of the Sands." The first portions were built in the 15th century and have been designated as an historic monument. It was damaged during both world wars and has had to undergo extensive renovations. Even today, numerous bullet holes are visible on the exterior walls.

- Malo-les-Bains Beach/Plage de Malo-les-Bains: A beautiful sandy beach which stretches for miles. The promenade offers numerous places to dine and even rent some equipment. Distance to the beach and promenade is best done by local bus service. Line C4 travels to Malo Beach from the train station. Also, check the Dunkirk bus timetable at **www.DKBus.com**

- Port Museum / Musée Portuaire de Dunkerque: Located in an appealing marina area, this maritime museum offers visitors the chance to go onboard several vessels and explore over 3 floors of exhibits including numerous ship models. A great destination for kids. It is roughly a 10-to-15-minute walk from the train station or the Belfry in the center of town. The museum's website is: **www.MuseePortuaire.com.**

- Dunkirk 1940 Operation Dynamo War Museum /Musée Dunkerque 1940: A comprehensive but somber museum devoted to 1he 1940 "Battle of Dunkirk" fought between the British and their allies against Nazi Germany. There were over 61,000 estimated casualties during this horrific event. The museum is near the Malo-les-Bains beach and it is easy to combine the two.

- Commonwealth War Memorial: An expansive cemetery honoring the British Commonwealth fighters including Canadians and Australians who lost their lives fighting here. The cemetery and memorial are slightly south of the town center, and it is not easy to walk to it. The best way to reach this site is by car.

Dunkirk Website: **www.Dunkerque-Toursime.fr.**

Boulogne-sur-Mer & Calais

Great alternatives to Dunkirk are the oceanside towns of Calais and Boulogne-sur-Mer. In each case, they are easy to reach by train, have expansive beaches, and delightful harbor areas to explore.

Lens:

Lens is a town of only 32,000 but is the home of an impressive extension of the noted Louvre Museum. Other attractions near this community are a mining museum and a war memorial in Vimy to fallen Canadians. When visiting by train, the Louvre-Lens Museum is often the site which first time visitors are drawn to.

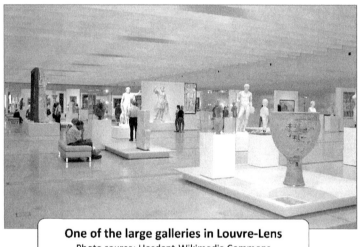

One of the large galleries in Louvre-Lens
Photo source: Hosdent-Wikimedia Commons

This is a pleasant town to visit, but there is little to attract the typical tourist. It is a former mining town and there are even high hills of mine tailings which overlook the town. When visiting here, consider focusing on the Louvre-Lens as it is easy to reach by local buses and presents a notable array of art and sculpture.

The Louvre-Lens Museum is a very modern facility and is part of the Louvre system. The collection here are all items from the main Louvre Museum in Paris. It was built to attract people who live in this area of France to a more convenient locale to view great works of art. Another goal of the museum had been to help build the otherwise depressed economy of the area.

Traveling to Lens:

Train travel time to Lens from Lille will be around 30 to 40 minutes. Trains depart from the Lille Flandres station. When arriving in Lens, the station is near the center of town, but not close to the art museum, so taking a bus in suggested. A bus stop is immediately outside the train station and bus #41 takes visitors to the Louvre-Lens stop.

Lens, France Website: www.Toursime-LensLievin.fr.

Roubaix or Tourcoing:

Near the border with Belgium are two appealing towns which are extremely easy to travel to for a day trip or even a short jaunt from Lille for a few hours. In each case, they may be reached by local train or metro and both towns provide pleasant explorations with some noteworthy attractions.

In the case of Roubaix, see chapter 8 for details on two of the leading attractions which came out of the area's history of textile design and manufacturing. This is also an excellent area to do some shopping. The long shopping street, Rue Mail de Lannoy, extends directly out from the train station.

Tourcoing offers a similar experience with an easy to reach city and pleasant shopping. One of the leading attractions here is Église Saint-Christophe, a neo-Gothic church dating back to the 11th century.

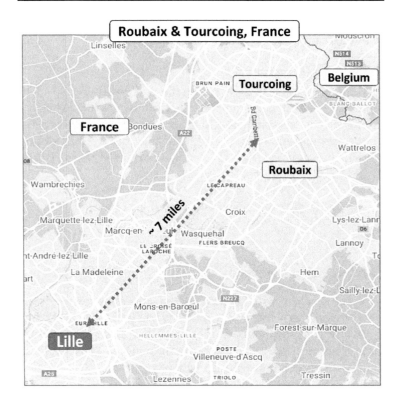

Traveling to Roubaix and Tourcoing:

- Roubaix: When traveling by public transportation from Lille, you have the advantage of being able to take local trains, the Metro/subway, and the light rail. For first-time visitors, taking the Metro to the Eurotéléport stop is recommended. This station lets you out in the heart of the city, near shopping, and it is close to the La Piscine Museum.

- Tourcoing: This town is also served by the three transportation systems of Metro, Light Rail, and Trains. Consider traveling by Metro or Light Rail to the Tourcoing Centre

120

stop. This is very close to the town's tourist office, shopping, and the large Église Saint-Christophe Catholic church.

City Websites:

- Roubaix: **www.RoubaixTourisme.com.**
- Tourcoing: **www.Tourcoing-Tourisme.com.**

Index

Starting-Point Guides

This guidebook on Lille is one of several current and planned *Starting-Point Guides*. Each book in the series is developed with the concept of using one enjoyable city as your basecamp and then exploring from there.

Zurich, Switzerland

A 2024 Starting-Point Travel Guide

Current guidebooks are for:

Austria:

- Salzburg, and the Salzburg area.

France:

- Bordeaux, Plus the surrounding Gironde River region
- Dijon Plus the Burgundy Region
- Lille and the Nord-Pas-de-Calais Area.
- Lyon, Plus the Saône and Rhône Confluence Region
- Nantes and the western Loire Valley.
- Reims and Épernay the heart of the Champagne Region.
- Strasbourg, and the central Alsace region.
- Toulouse, and the Haute-Garonne area.

Germany:

- Cologne & Bonn
- Dresden and the Saxony State
- Stuttgart and the and the Baden-Württemberg area.

Spain:

- <u>Camino Easy</u>: A mature walker's guide to the popular Camino de Santiago trail.
- <u>Toledo:</u> The City of Three Cultures

Sweden:

- <u>Gothenburg</u> Plus the Västra Götaland region.

Switzerland:

- <u>Geneva</u>, Including the Lake Geneva area.
- <u>Lucerne</u>, Including the Lake Lucerne area.
- <u>Zurich</u> – And the Lake Zurich area.

Updates on these and other titles may be found on the author's Facebook page at:

<u>www.Facebook.com/BGPreston.author</u>

Feel free to use this Facebook page to provide feedback and suggestions to the author or email to: <u>cincy3@gmail.com</u>

LILLE

Printed in Great Britain
by Amazon